MAK~E~. *ing*

IT. ^

HAPPEN.

The Ultimate Guide to **SELLING**

SPENCER **LODGE**

Dedication

*Dedicated to all of the people willing to take risks,
overcome huge obstacles and create a life that they're proud of.*

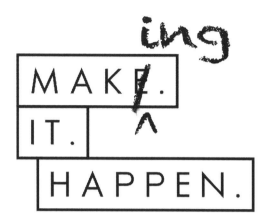

MAK~E~ing.
IT. ^
HAPPEN.

The Ultimate Guide to **SELLING**

SPENCER **LODGE**

About Spencer Lodge

Having recently been voted as one of the Top 100 Most Influential People in Dubai, there's no denying that Spencer Lodge has been making waves in the international financial services and sales industry for many decades. With over 25 years' experience, he's personally trained thousands of people during his career and has helped build some of the largest and most successful direct sales forces, delivering expert results for his clients.

After dedicating his career to building businesses and training employees to achieve their full potential, in 2015 Spencer decided that it was time to spread his wealth of knowledge internationally, and Make-It-Happen University was born. Through this online platform, Spencer shares his secrets to success, and gives anyone who needs to create revenue —including entrepreneurs and professional salespeople — every tool they need to succeed.

Spencer's can-do attitude has seen him achieve some incredible feats, most recently climbing Mount Kilimanjaro and cycling over 1,000 kilometres from London to Geneva to raise money for children with special needs. He has also summited past Everest Base Camp to Kala Patthar – 5,800 metres above sea level. In the future, Spencer plans to undertake further adventures to raise money for causes close to his heart.

For Spencer, winning isn't everything – it's the only thing. Once he sets his mind to something, there's nothing that he can't do. He's a devoted husband, a loving father, an adventurer, a public speaker, a business leader, a philanthropist – who has donated over $1 million for children in Africa born with HIV –and an author.

facebook.com/makeithappensl

instagram.com/makeithappensl

Acknowledgments

A lot goes into writing a book, and I'd like to take a moment to acknowledge the people who have been a part of this journey. I would like to thank Karen Rogerson for putting my thoughts into words and helping me write this book.

During my career I've been influenced by brilliant minds such as Tony Robbins, Gary Vaynerchuk, Russell Brunson, Zig Ziglar, and my own personal mentor, David Shillingis, who taught me how to sell. I hope that everyone who reads this book is inspired and reminded that you can do anything that you put your mind to.

Contents

PART I

Introduction to Sales

The Personality of a Salesperson

"We are what we repeatedly do. Excellence, then, is not an act, but a habit."
– Aristotle (Greek philosopher)

Most people believe that in order to make it as a successful salesperson, you have to be an extrovert. Although my parents always claimed that I had 'the gift of the gab', I wouldn't necessarily classify myself as having an extroverted personality. I like my own company; I prefer not to go out to crowded bars and restaurants; and I wake up at 4:30 a.m. every morning so that I can enjoy some quiet time before the rest of the world gets up. However, if you put me in front of a group of Eskimos, my parents would assure you that I'd be able to sell them snow.

Growing up I was just an average kid from an average family, living in average England. There was nothing special about my life and I certainly wasn't born with a silver spoon in my mouth. My parents got divorced, and my father lost his business when I was only a youngster. My mum had to work two jobs in order to keep a roof over our head, and my dad had to rebuild himself and his business from the ground up. Although this might not sound like the ideal upbringing, there was always a lot of love in my home, and seeing how hard my parents had to work in order to rebuild their lives made me realise that, if you put a lot of effort in, there's nothing that you can't take on. If you have determination, you can achieve anything you set your mind to!

I've often been asked what I would be doing if I wasn't in sales. Having spent over 27 years in the industry, it's hard to imagine doing anything else, but before I started selling, I was dead set on being a ski-instructor! I'd always been sport obsessed, and back then nothing made me happier than spending my days on the slopes. This, however, didn't sit well with my mother, who insisted that I needed to have a 'proper career'. Although I didn't even know what a 'salesman' did, I agreed to go to an interview to appease my parents. Little did I know back then that sales would change my life forever.

I've always had a hunter's attitude to life. I see what I want, and I go after it. And, after being introduced to the world of sales, I knew for sure that that's what I wanted to do. When I first started out, my mentor, David Shillingis, provided training to a group of us from 06:00 a.m. until 07:30 a.m. every morning. The job was in London so it meant having to wake up at 04:30 a.m. and leave my house no later than 05:00 a.m. every day. If you didn't arrive at the training on time, you weren't allowed in, but because I found the sessions so inspiring, I was always front and centre. I was prepared to eat, sleep, drink, and breathe sales if it meant becoming the best salesperson out there!

Going back to what I said earlier about not needing an extroverted personality – I don't believe that all great salespeople have to be extro-verted, but I do think that they have to have certain characteristics in common. If you're in sales just to make a quick buck, and you believe that success is going to come easy, then you're in the wrong industry! I've come across so many people in my career who are selling things that they don't believe in, and pretending to be people who they're not. Being a great salesperson is actually about being yourself, believing in your product, and trying your best to help others. You have to be achievement orientated, optimistic, driven, curious, and have good people skills and a tough skin.

Top tips: Common character traits of a great salesperson

1. **Be an optimist:** People naturally gravitate towards positive people, as optimists choose to see the possibilities in every situation. By consciously being more positive, you'll find yourself attracting more clients, and you'll be more motivated to do the job.
2. **Have a conscience:** If you don't believe in what you're selling, then you shouldn't be selling it. The psychology behind sales is incredibly complex, and if you don't honestly believe that your product or service can help the lives of others, then you shouldn't be selling it.
3. **Be results driven:** Set your targets high and then achieve them. Great salespeople don't do anything half-assed! Be all in at all times!

Why Sales Skills Are Necessary

"It is not your customer's job to remember you. It is your obligation and responsibility to make sure they don't have the chance to forget you."
– Patricia Fripp (American author)

All successful people have something in common: they know how to sell. Having coached and mentored hundreds of successful people over the years, I am very certain that these individuals will all tell you that without solid sales skills, success is almost impossible.

Everyone needs to know how to sell. Selling is a prerequisite in life. Whether you're a young professional, someone going for a job interview, or the CEO of a company, if you don't know how to market yourself, you're not going to make a very good impression on the people you meet.

Selling is all about persuading, convincing, and negotiating. It's essentially about making a fantastic first impression, being a great listener, and ultimately helping people find a solution to their need.

If you're a CEO, then you're selling your company or organisation. If you're an entrepreneur, then you're selling your ideas to potential stakeholders. And if you're a young professional going for an interview, then you're selling yourself and the skills that you can offer to your potential employer. So having great sales skills is essential for everyone!

Gaining sales skills will help you bring in investors, win financing, line up deals, land clients, and even help you to convince an employer to give you your dream job. Understanding the sales process, and how to build long-term relationships, is incredibly important, regardless of the industry or career you choose. If you put in the effort to learn the tools of the trade, or spend some time in a direct sales role, you'll see your success skyrocket! Sales skills will ensure that you're able to persuade, negotiate, and operate in the world of commerce.

The skills that I've learnt in the sales industry over the years have taught me self-discipline and persistence, along with how to negotiate, how to close a deal, how to stay focused, and how to communicate with anyone about anything!

When you go for a job interview what do you think the employer is looking at? Your credentials? Your university degree? Your experience?

For me personally, when it comes to recruiting new members to join my team, I look for a combination of all of the above. In addition to this, however, the candidate has to have a phenomenal attitude and be able to convince me why I need them, and why they would make a significant difference to my business. If they're unable to sell themselves to me, then there's no way that I can count on them to sell themselves to anyone else.

Have you ever heard of the elevator pitch? In an elevator pitch, you need to explain what you do, and why you do it, in no more than 30 seconds. For this to make an impact, you need to decide on the key points that you want to convey, and how you can do it in that short space of time. Whether you're selling a product, or yourself, it's imperative to have a number of elevator pitches handy.

The importance of having a sales mindset is clear when you consider the large number of tech companies that have failed in recent years. A lot of these entrepreneurs will claim that they couldn't raise enough money, but if you have a great idea then you should be selling that idea.

If you aren't raising enough money, then either you're not selling your idea or services fast enough, or you're not selling it in the correct way. It doesn't matter how great your idea is if you're not selling it to anyone. A lot of people who start up new businesses will face this challenge. While some new small companies may thrive, most of them will go bust in their first year. This is because the people who set up these small businesses don't understand the value of selling and the skills that are needed to help their company grow.

Selling will create revenue, and if you create revenue you can keep yourself moving forward. If you're going to set up a business and are already going through the hassle of legally setting it up, buying stock, or getting products manufactured, then it's of vital importance to know the value of selling.

Sales will keep your business alive. If you've got a good idea or concept for a business, then I urge you to invest proper time in learning how to sell. This will ensure that you know how to approach the right people, and get them to buy into your idea.

Top tips: How to make a great first impression

1. **Practise your elevator pitch**: First impressions matter. Practise your elevator pitch at home by speaking to yourself in the mirror. Introduce yourself, and say what you do and why you do it. Think of what makes you interesting, and what other people might find interesting about you, and then highlight these things.

2. **What makes your idea unique?** Whether you're selling a product, your company, a service, or yourself, you need to know what makes the thing you're trying to sell special. If it doesn't add value to other people's lives, then why would people be interested in buying it? What does your product have that separates it from other similar products out there?

3

Appearance

"You can never be overdressed or overeducated."
– Oscar Wilde (Irish poet)

There are too many businesses out there that don't take dress code seriously these days. These companies encourage their employees to dress freely or casually for comfort. Call me old fashioned, but I believe that first impressions matter. And what kind of first impression are you making in your baggy track-pants and sneakers? A CEO wouldn't trust a person dressed like that with their petty cash, never mind their business!

In the sales industry, you are not only selling premium products or services, but you're also selling yourself, so it's imperative to always look your best. You never know when you will be required to meet with a big client, or with someone from outside your company. What you've got to remember is that you represent your organisation, and your image to the outside world will be the image that people remember when they think of your company.

Your appearance and business attire need to be professional at all times. I'd go so far to say that the image that you portray to others could indirectly mean the difference between securing a new deal, contract, or sale and losing the opportunity completely. Make sure that you're always the best-dressed person in the room. Dressing to impress shows that you mean business, and will ensure that you are taken seriously.

An example I always think of when it comes to dress code is a woman named Sarah. Ten years ago, Sarah walked into my office for a job interview. She had platinum-blonde hair, and her outfit choice left half of the men in the office with their tongues hanging on the floor. Although Sarah had a great attitude, and I knew that she'd be able to do a fantastic job, I told her that I couldn't hire her looking the way that she did. Don't get me wrong, she looked great, but I knew the men in the office wouldn't take her seriously unless she looked more professional. Sarah took note of what I said, and the next time I saw her, she was wearing an impressive suit, and I knew then that she meant business. I hired her on the spot, and she's been my PA ever since, playing an instrumental role in many of my businesses.

Ever heard of the saying, "Don't dress for the job you have; dress for the job you want"? If you want to be the CEO of a multi-million dollar empire one day, then why not dress like one now? Always think bigger, and aim higher. My advice to anyone starting out in the sales industry is to invest in some great quality suits. Even if you're not making the big bucks yet, you need to look like you are!

When you meet a prospect for the first time, your shoes and your belt should match, your shoes should be polished, your trousers and jacket should be pressed and you should exude the type of confidence that commands attention. Looking like a million dollars will always work in your favour.

Top tips: Appearance

1. **Be prepared:** Planning your outfit the night before will help you look more presentable. Often, when we're rushing in the morning we don't take the proper time or care in choosing the right thing to wear. I've often seen people wearing stained or marked garments that look like they came straight out of their laundry basket. Don't be this person! Attention to detail makes the world of difference.

2. **Quality over quantity:** Invest in quality office apparel. You can never go wrong with a well-tailored suit in classic colours such as black and navy.

3. **Cover up:** Less isn't always more. Clothes that are too revealing, too tight, too short, and too out there might get you noticed – but not for the right reasons! I'm not suggesting you pitch up at your next meeting looking like a convent nun, but for goodness' sake, make sure that not all of your goods are on display.

4

The Sales Process

"Without hustle, your talent will only get you so far."
– Gary Vaynerchuk (entrepreneur, author, speaker
and internet personality)

W e've already discussed just how important it is to look the part when meeting someone for the first time. And something that goes hand in hand with appearance is your personal hygiene. If you're the type of guy or girl who tends to get clammy hands, then make sure that you wash your hands in the bathroom before you meet your prospect. Limp and sweaty hands are never well received!

In order to present your products and services in the most effective way, it's crucial that you make a great first impression. When you meet your prospect, be sure to give them a firm handshake, and a warm, friendly smile when introducing yourself.

Remember that a hand over the top means that you're taking control and a hand underneath is taking a vulnerable approach, so keep that hand in a vertical position while you tell your prospect how great it is to meet them.

This may seem simple, but I've seen so many salespeople fail at getting their prospect over the finish line, simply because they messed up their introduction.

Top tips: Introductions

1. Make sure you look the part
2. Wash your hands before you meet your prospect
3. Properly introduce yourself with a firm handshake

Once you've made your introductions, engage with your prospect. It's important to remember that they aren't interested in your personal stories, so you might want to keep that anecdote about your cat's latest antics to yourself for now.

What people do care about is themselves – so keep the conversation focused on them! This is where open-ended questions come in. These are questions that your prospect has to answer with anything other than a "yes" or "no". Open-ended questions start with who, what, why, when, where, or how.

These types of questions are a great way to elicit information from a new prospect. In this way, you can register and log that detail for further dealings with the client. It is absolutely essential that in that first meeting, the prospect likes you and thinks of you as a credible person or business contact. If you keep the conversation focused on yourself, or if you don't ask engaging questions, your prospect might lose interest. Therefore, asking open-ended questions is key to this part of the sales process.

By doing these things, you will put your prospect at ease. People are often suspicious that we're just trying to sell them something they don't need. Put your prospect at ease and break through their barriers, but be careful not to overstep your mark and talk about subjects that might make them uncomfortable.

Start by building rapport and putting them at ease with the following rule for conversations: Work – Social – Family.

As your first port of call, ask open-ended questions about what they do professionally. Examples of these questions would include:

"How long have you worked for this company, Mr/Ms Smith?"
"What type of job do you do?"
"Why did you choose to work in this industry?"

Get your prospect to talk about their work, as people are generally quite happy to talk about what they do for a living, especially those who are passionate about what they do. I can guarantee you that if you ask open-ended questions, the person you're meeting with will find you interesting, even though they know nothing about you.

Remember to show real interest in what they are saying. It is important that you don't fake it, but rather be genuinely attentive. They are your prospective clients, after all. They might not be willing to buy from you today, but you have an opportunity to sell to them today. If you do all those things correctly, then you'll give yourself a fighting chance to make that happen.

Once you have asked questions about work, and got an understanding of why your prospect does what they do, you can then move on to the social questions. Ask open-ended questions about what they do when they're not at work, what kind of hobbies or interests they have, whether they are part of a social club or a sport team, for example. Try to understand what your prospect does in their spare time and what they are passionate about. If you're listening to what they do in their spare time, it might also give you the opportunity to get introductions to other potential prospects. Always remember to listen intently and to store that information for later use.

Once you've asked your prospect about their work and social life, you can then move on to learning more about their family. Ask open-ended questions like *"How old are your children?"*, *"Where do they go to school?"*, or *"Why did you choose that school?"*. If your prospect tells you the names of any of their family members, make sure to remember them! The prospect will be very impressed if you mention those names later on.

In order for us to establish great rapport with clients, we have to ask the right questions. If you know that your prospect has kids, then you'll be able to sell them an education savings plan, or a family car. If, however, you learn that your prospect is single, then you could get them interested in a two-door sports car. Knowing your prospect well will ensure that you're able to offer them the product or service that's right for them.

Top tips: Asking questions

1. Ask questions on the prospect's Work, Social and Family life for about 15 minutes before resuming with the remainder of your meeting. Remember to ask open-ended questions that start with who, what, why, when, where, or how.

Once you've managed to get to a place where you know more about your prospect, then you need to focus on understanding the psychology and the dynamic at hand. The prospect may be thinking, *"This guy's trying to sell me and I don't want to get sold"* or *"I don't have much time. I hope they're really quick"* or *"I hope I'm not obliged to buy something. I'm not sure I can trust this person."* These feelings are absolutely natural and are normal for every single prospect you talk to, but if you're not aware of them, you'll carry on bulldozing your way through the process.

It's really important that we take care to understand the psychology and the dynamic that exists between the prospect and the salesperson. If you get it right, it's going to be great. If you get it wrong, it's going to be a problem, so make sure that you're sensitive to that.

Remember that the fact that they're meeting you means that there's an interest. And it's your job to take them from the small amount of interest that they may have, to convincing them that you're the right professional for them. Your job is to get them over those barriers so that they have complete faith in the fact that you're the person that they should be dealing with on this matter. You've got to increase their level of interest and trust. If you knock down their psychological barriers and take away their fears, you'll be in a much better place as you move through the sales process.

It's important to remember that our clients are going to have fears and it's critical to understand what these fears are.

Some of them could be:

- The fear of making a decision
- The fear of being ripped off
- The fear of financial insecurity, where they'll be asking themselves, "Can I afford something like this?"
- The fear of feeling pressured (even if you're not pressuring them at all)
- The fear of not having enough time
- The fear of feeling obligated to reciprocate (often if prospects spend time with you they'll feel obligated to buy something from you).
- The fear of saying no.

Be aware of the fears that your prospect might have, and the process that they'll have to go through when dealing with you. If you learn how to handle these fears, it'll make a big difference.

When I was selling financial services in my early twenties, I dealt with a married couple in Holland who told me that they were were reluctant to make a big decision about a savings programme without first consulting the Lord. I offered to step outside so that they could have some time alone to pray. I called my boss at the time, and told him about the strange situation. After a while they came to fetch me and said that they had prayed and felt at peace, and decided to purchase the savings plan. I replied saying: "*Well that's good, because even Jesus saves*". We laughed and they've been clients of mine ever since!

Once you've built a rapport with your prospect; asked them open-ended questions about work, their social life and family; and eased some of their fears; you'll move on to your fact-finding exercise. Once again, this entails asking questions!

Let's say, for example, that you're selling your client financial services. If you're talking to your prospect about their children and their education, it's important to understand whether or not university is a priority for them (some people want their children to go to university, but for others this isn't that important). I would ask the following questions:

- *"What school did you choose for your daughter to go to?"*
- *"Why did you choose that school?"*
- *"How did you come to that decision?"*
- *"Tell me more about what type of school it is and what fees you pay currently?"*
- *"What are your plans regarding university for your child?"*

If I were discussing life insurance with my client, then I'd ask questions such as:

- *"What kind of allowances or preparations have you made to make sure that your family has enough money if you pass away?"*
- *"What plans have you got in place to make sure that your family is protected?"*

These kinds of questions are good fact-finding questions, where you can establish where your prospect is and where they'd like to be. Some people might be thinking a lot about the future, but others aren't really worried about it. There is no point in guessing. Rather ask questions and learn. Keep probing until you find a need that your prospect has. It's important that we ask great questions, and gather as much information as we can so that we can move on to the next gear of the sale. If we haven't asked the right questions, then we haven't established the need, and if we haven't established the need, then what are we going to sell?

Top tips: Common mistakes to avoid

1. **Misinterpreting fears**: It's your job to understand exactly what your prospect's fears are and why they have them.
2. **Not approaching problems as opportunities**: See every problem as an opportunity. Remember that every negative situation can be turned around. A positive attitude is a winning attitude.
3. **Telling your prospect "I don't know"**: Make sure that you know your subject well enough so that you always have an answer. You need to be an expert in your field.

5

Commission Isn't a Bad Word

"If you aim at nothing, you will hit it every time."
– Zig Ziglar (American author, salesman, and motivational speaker)

People often ask me how I've made a success living off commission alone. Are you kidding me? Commission must be the single greatest way of earning an income! A lot of people might argue that a salary is a safer option. They'll tell you all about their monthly expenses that they need to cover, and why it's better to get a regular income every month. Well, in my opinion, you'll never achieve big success by playing it safe, nor will you achieve it by receiving the same mediocre salary every month.

With commission you get paid for what you do, what you deliver, and what you're worth. Commission is so much better than a salary. You can earn far more money by working on commission, and you'll also have that much more job satisfaction at the end of the month. The only catch – it's not for the lazy! If you want to see big figures rolling in, then you'd better be prepared to put the hard work in. If you set your targets high, and stay committed, then you shouldn't have any problem. This way you're in control of your own income, your own bank balance, and your future success. Commission isn't a bad word – it's when you get something in return for doing a good job!

Although the term 'commission' relates to a form of payment for doing something, there are also different forms of commission that exist. Commission is also when you get a pay raise, when you are promoted, or even when you make a new friend. Commission is determined by what you put in. Think about it this way: even your love life is a commission. If you're married and you aren't invested in it, then you're not going to get anything out. But if you put work into the relationship, then you're going to get love back and that love is a commission too. Don't underestimate that. Understand the importance of commission in all aspects of your life. Don't attach the word just to money made by making a sale. Take a step back and analyse your life so that you're able to see all the areas in your life where you earn commission.

There have been so many people over the years who have told me that they couldn't do what I do and that they wouldn't be able to work on commission. But of course you can! If you commit, work hard and put the hours in, then you're going to get a lot out, whether that's in your job or your private life.

With commission sales, there is no cap on your earnings, meaning you can thrive financially when things are going well. Clearly define your targets so that you achieve excellent results on a regular basis.

Top tips: Commission

1. **Stop fearing commission:** Commission is a fantastic way to make money. Stop convincing yourself that it's a bad thing and commit to working hard so that you can see great results.
2. **Manage your money:** You never know what the future

holds. Things may be good today, and the money could be pouring in, but what happens if something changes that? Always make allowances for your future, and never spend money that you don't have. If you're planning on making a big purchase, then rather wait until you have all the money upfront.

PART II

Perfect Prospecting

6

What Is Prospecting?

"Keep your sales pipeline full by prospecting continuously. Always have more people to see than you have time to see them."
– Brian Tracy (motivational public speaker and self-development author)

Many newbie salespeople get confused between prospecting and networking. Essentially, prospecting refers to exploration, and in sales, prospecting is the search for potential customers. At this stage it's not about selling. The aim of prospecting is to find qualified leads and people or organisations that are able to purchase your product or service.

Although many salespeople will tell you that prospecting is the worst part of their job, it plays a crucial and essential role. Without prospects, you wouldn't have anyone to sell to. Never underestimate the importance of being a really good prospector. I was once asked if I would choose between a really good prospector who was an average salesperson and an average prospector who was a really good salesperson. I would tell you every single time that when it comes to employing salespeople, if they're great prospectors then they're going to do well. If they know how to get prospects and generate leads, then there will always be ways to make money, be successful, and satisfy clients' desires.

Finding and connecting with prospects can be done in a number of different ways. Back in the old days, prospecting was done via door knocking and cold calling. Nowadays, thanks to advances in technology, many organisations are investing in digital and social media to find their leads, and it's much easier to find prospects. But it's still important to be aware of all the different ways to prospect, so that you can find what works best for you.

Although prospecting can be tough and uncomfortable at times, research shows that your attitude and actions will determine how successful you are. You need to develop a healthy attitude when it comes to prospecting, and then take action. Even if your sales are through the roof, you won't be able to sustain this kind of success without a constant influx of new prospects. Discovering the key to perfect prospecting means discovering the key to success!

7

Networking

"Networking is not about just connecting people. It's about connecting people with people, people with ideas, and people with opportunities."
- Michele Jennae (creativity coach)

The ability to network is one of the most important skills any entrepreneur or salesperson can have. Essentially, the definition of networking, according to the Oxford Dictionary, is "Interacting with others to exchange information and develop professional or social contacts". But in the sales industry it's so much more than that. Many people go to networking events, but very few people know how to network effectively.

Networking is about more than just getting out and meeting people. Networking is about introducing people who you know to other people. You must have heard the saying, "It's who you know, not what you know", and this couldn't be more apt if your goal is to be an excellent salesperson. If you want to be the best, then you'll have to build the best network possible.

Think about your personal network for a minute: these are the people that you know. Then think about all the people that your existing contacts know. Think of the ways that you can meet and get exposed to these people, and how can you build your network through the networks of others.

The best way to succeed at networking is to ensure that you have solid networking skills, that you're putting yourself out there, and that you're attending relevant industry events, gatherings, seminars, and functions.

Instead of sitting at home watching TV on a Friday night, you should be out there building a name for yourself and growing your network.

I've had a lot of people tell me that they initially feel quite uncomfortable in these networking situations, and it's normal to feel this way at first. But getting out there, shaking hands, introducing yourself, and making new connections is going to be very beneficial for you. After a while of doing this, it will start to feel more natural.

The people who you meet at these events are there for the same reason that you're there – to network! If you bear that in mind, you'll already feel more at ease. At the end of the evening, you would have met at least four or five new people and you'll feel motivated and buzzed. You never know when these contacts will come in handy, so be sure to get their names, numbers, email addresses, and even their social media details, so that you can stay connected.

You can learn a great deal about a person from their social media pages. You'll be able to see their likes, hobbies, and what they do outside of work. In addition to this, you are also a lot more likely to get hold of someone through social media these days than you are on email.

Top tips: How to network

1. **Set a goal to meet two or three people at each event you attend:** Whether you're at a seminar, a networking function, a birthday party, or an industry event, it's important to make a point of speaking to all the people who you don't know. Greet everyone, and introduce yourself. So many of us fall into the trap of always speaking to the same old acquaintances. Don't let this be you.

2. **Attend one or two new groups on a weekly basis:** Another great way to make a new set of contacts is to attend business organisation meetings or activities that interest you. Some examples include the chamber of commerce, the arts council, a sports club, or a society.

3. **Always carry your business cards:** You never know when you're going to meet a key contact, so make sure you always have your business cards with you.

8

Door Knocking

"You just can't beat the person who never gives up."
- Babe Ruth (American baseball player)

I n the movie *The Karate Kid*, the protagonist's first lesson is cleaning and waxing his master's car. You may remember the line "Wax on, wax off". Although I didn't have to wax any cars at the start of my career, I had a great mentor who bore many similarities to Mr Miyagi. Every day I had to knock on 100 doors and get 100 phone numbers. If I didn't get that many, I wasn't allowed to come back to the office. Once I had collected those numbers, I had to call all 100 of them. This was my daily routine. No ifs, no buts, no maybes.

At the time, I didn't see the point of these activities, but subconsciously my boss was teaching me some very valuable lessons. Perseverance is so important, and if you can't follow through on simple tasks, then you're not going to experience the kind of success that you want.

Door knocking is when you go out of your office and introduce yourself to people at every address you go to.

If you're selling something that's relevant to retailers, for example, then you would go into every shop in the area and introduce yourself to the manager of each store. If you are selling office supplies, then you would go to different businesses and ask to speak to the person responsible for this. The point is to introduce yourself, build a bit of rapport, and establish whether or not your product or service could be of interest to that person.

It's a tough way of doing things, and is also quite time consuming, but if this is how you or your company chooses to go about prospecting, then it's essential to get it right. Once again, it's important to follow these steps:

- Make sure that you look presentable.
- Don't forget about your personal hygiene, especially since you're going to be meeting people face to face.
- Ensure you have a positive attitude because the process can wear you down otherwise.

Remember that you're going to get some 'noes' when you door knock. But when you get these 'noes', it's important to see them as 'noes' that are going to lead to a 'yes'. You will get some resistance, but this is when you should use your charm, your charisma, and your personality to engage with people who you've never met before so that they can provide you with the information that you need. You can then turn these people into prospects. If you can master this method, then all the other methods of prospecting will be a lot easier. Work ethic is really important and your full commitment is imperative.

Top tips: How to door knock like a pro

1. **Watch your body language:** Some people might be a bit suspicious of a stranger standing on their porch, or coming into their office. If your body language is unfriendly, they

probably won't let you inside. Don't cross your arms, pace, or stand abrasively in front of them, as this might come across as intimidating and aggressive. Stand a few steps back and have a welcoming smile when you approach people.

2. **Introduce yourself:** A lot of people don't like engaging with strangers. Most people will want to know four things straight away: Who are you? Where are you from? What are you doing here? When will you leave? Answer these questions straight away, and they'll immediately be more at ease.

3. **Dress for success:** Would you invite someone dressed like a homeless person into your home or office? Chances are you wouldn't! Make sure you look professional and polished when going door to door.

9

Cold Calling

"Act as if what you do makes a difference. It does."
- William James (American philosopher)

Whether you like it or not, calling people is a part of business. Everyone has to cold call at some point in his or her career, regardless of whether or not you're in the sales industry. If you're in public relations, you'll have to call journalists to pitch your client's story. If you want the job of your dreams, you'll have to call the organisation to find out if there are any vacancies. If you're starting your own business, you'll have to call companies in order to find clients.

I've had many people argue that cold calling is still important, even if new methods of making contact are more relevant in today's day and age. And while I do believe that everyone should know how to make calls, and sell over the telephone, I don't think that you should sit in the office for ten hours a day sorting through cold data and making cold calls in the hope that someone might take a bite. There are other prospecting strategies that work better in my opinion, but since this chapter deals with prospecting, it's still important to know how to factor cold calling into your business, and make a success of it. Below I'll be outlining some of the best tips that I've learnt over the years.

Is cold calling still relevant?

There are more mobile phones than there are people on the planet. According to a recent study done by the University College of Northern Denmark (UCN), an average of 12.4 billion calls are made every day (and that's not even factoring in the calls that are made over WhatsApp and other messaging platforms). A person's mobile device is never far from them, which means that the easiest way to make contact with a prospect is to call them. You could go out and see them in person, but this takes a lot of time. That's why a lot of business nowadays is done over the phone. Although cold calling isn't my favourite prospecting strategy, it's important to know how to engage with people who you haven't met before.

Generating leads is vital in business and cold calling is a great way of prospecting. I've been building businesses over the past 25 years, and we've always included cold calling as part of our strategy. When I first started in the sales industry, my job was to knock on 100 doors and then cold call 100 numbers each and every day. Did I love doing this? No! But it was a tool that I had to use. Don't hide behind the fact that you don't like doing something. It's part of the job. If you accept it and embrace it, then it can work for you.

What other industries should use cold calling?

- If you're in the automotive industry and need to sell cars, you can cold call prospects to find out if they're interested in a new vehicle.
- If you have a start-up and need to drum up new business, cold calling is one way to find potential clients.
- If you're a real estate agent who needs to sell properties, then you can contact people to ask if they're interested in selling their house.

- If you're organising a seminar, then you're going to have to call people to invite them to the event.

Let's take a look at some of the reasons why people don't like cold calling:

• There must be an easier way

People want to believe that there's an easier way to create leads. But how much easier do you get than obtaining a name and number and calling that person after you've done some research?

• You don't want to put people on the spot

Perhaps you don't like engaging with people that you don't know. You don't want to pressure people or make them feel uncomfortable. But unless you pick the phone up and start calling people, you're not going to be successful.

• The fear of rejection

The number one reason why people don't like cold calling is because they fear rejection. In the world of sales however, rejection is just a part of the game. Every job has aspects to it that you don't enjoy. What's the worst that could happen? They might say no and hang up, but it certainly won't kill you!

• You'd rather spend money on advertising

A lot of people tell me that they'd rather spend money on advertising than on calling people. If you're a small company that hasn't been in business for long, then this might not pan out well, especially as the way that people consume adverts has changed dramatically. People don't watch television anymore, hardly anyone reads newspapers, and advertising on online platforms is often ignored. So how is advertising going to be more beneficial than picking up the phone?

Cold calling statistics

- **63% of people don't like cold calling**

Sixty-three percent of salespeople will tell you that the thing they like least about their job is cold calling. That would mean that 37% don't actually mind it. This 37% are most likely the top performers in their company.

- **9% of the people you contact for the first time will be interested**

Ninety-one percent of buyers never respond to an unsolicited enquiry. But this means that 9% do! Almost 10% of the people who you contact will be interested, so if it means calling ten people to get one who will respond positively, then do it.

- **12% of buyers will do business with you from a cold call**

It's inevitable that you're going to get some noes, but you should look at the positives and focus on the people who are willing to do business with you.

When making a cold call, it's important to define what a contact really is. A contact is a person who is either a decision maker or an influencer in their company. In sales, you want to sell to someone who can make a decision. If you're calling up a company and can't get through to the decision maker, then try an influencer.

Sometimes an influencer is a PA, or sometimes it's someone in a senior management position. Try and understand who the person is, and make sure that you're making contact with the right person. There's no point in calling up a company and wasting time speaking to someone who can't help you in your potential sale.

For example, if you're selling insurance to young married couples, then you don't want to be talking to their aunt and uncle. However, if you can't seem to get through to the right person, then you can always ask the person you're talking to if they know of anyone who would be interested in your product or service. As a salesperson, you should always be thinking of ways to get more introductions.

I often speak about how important it is to do the numbers, and that's especially important when making cold calls. You need to know exactly what's involved so that you are aware of what you have to do in order to get to where you need to go.

It's important that you know how many calls you need to make in order to get the result you're looking for. This makes the exercise a lot simpler and easier.

But if you haven't done the maths, then it's just going to be a thankless task and you're going to spend hours going through cold data and more hours making cold calls without knowing what your exact goal is, and how close you are to reaching it.

For example, if you know that you need to make 10 sales this week, and it takes you 10 calls to find one prospect, then you know that you have to call a minimum of 100 people. But that's only if your closing ratio is 100%, of course. If, however, you don't manage to close all of your prospects, then you'll have to up the number of cold calls you make to correctly reflect your statistics.

An important thing that you'll have to do before you can start calling these people is make a list. This may seem like common sense, but I've dealt with many salespeople who just call prospects as they go, without sticking to a list or formula. It's important to know who your target market is, and how you're going to approach them.

If you're stuck, a good place to start when making a contact list is LinkedIn. This social media platform for professionals is very powerful because it gives you information about people's job titles, their work history, and what company they work for currently.

You can also build lists using the names of people who you've spoken to in the past that didn't do business with you at the time, or perhaps include details of past clients who now do business with another company.

If you've changed industries, for example you used to sell cars and you're now selling real estate, you can contact all the people you sold cars to in the past and tell them that you're now in real estate. There will be a level of familiarity there since they purchased something from you in the past.

There are also companies that sell lists and data. So if you don't have enough time to do the research yourself, and need some assistance in getting hold of people who would benefit from your product or services, reach out to these companies for some assistance. If you choose to go this route, then make sure that these lists are updated.

Do some research on the company you want to do business with:

It's important to research the person or business before you call them. Find out exactly what they do and what business they're in. Find out what they're doing, and what they're doing well. Perhaps the company has been in the news recently, or put out a press release. It's imperative to know everything that you can about a company, before you call them. It's also important to understand what your contact's role and influence is within their company.

It's essential to note, however, that you shouldn't criticise your contact based on the information you find when researching. For example, if you were selling web services, you shouldn't call up a contact and tell them that they have a terrible website. This will offend them, and they'll immediately shut down. Instead speak about all the positives, and how you can assist them in making the website even better.

Get a good understanding of what the company's USPs are:

It's vital to understand the company's unique selling points (USPs). What is the company doing differently? What is their approach to market and how do they get their clients? The more intelligence that you have on this company, the easier it's going to be for you when you make your phone call. A good way of understanding this is by studying their competitors. Make a list of everything that they're doing differently, and what makes them stand out.

Find personal connections you might have within the company:

When approaching the company, try and find any personal contacts that you might have to leverage into this company. You might have connections on LinkedIn who are customers of the company that you're trying to get into, for example. If you can call the CEO of the company and tell him that you know the Managing Director of one of their big clients, then this will help you. Connections are everything in this industry. Having a connection in common makes you appear more trustworthy. No one wants to do business with a complete stranger.

Connect with influencers inside the company:

Try and connect on LinkedIn and other platforms with influencers inside the company that you're trying to do business with. If there are people within the company who you are connected to and who can influence company decisions, then having them as connections will work in your favour.

Script everything!

If you're going to be making phone calls then you need a script. Do not wing it! It will make you sound unprepared and unprofessional. Your script should be your road map. Write out the script, practise the script, and role play the situation until you are polished and you know it off by heart. Remember that you've probably got about 12 seconds to make an impact. This impact will come from your energy, your enthusiasm, your passion, and your commitment. When you need to make a good impression on a prospect quickly, you need to give it everything you've got. It's also vital that you believe what you're saying, and are passionate about what you're selling. A lot of salespeople don't like to role play before doing a cold call, but it's something that you've got to do. Think about an actor in a movie – he learns his lines, rehearses his lines, and then it still takes him a couple of takes to get it right. If you've got a pitch, then role play it with someone. Record it and then listen back. You'll hear the changes as you improve.

Prepare for objections:

Objections are inevitable, so be sure to be ready for them. Think about every single objection you could come across and write them all down.

The next step is to come up with three different answers for each objection. Try to think of objections relevant to your industry. If, for example, you're in financial services, then a possible objection could be, *"I can't afford this package right now,"* or, *"Your competitor offers a similar savings plan at a cheaper rate"*. For every objection you think of, make sure you have strong responses.

Learn, memorise, and rehearse every response so when you do come across an objection, you can combat it straight away and handle it assertively. You need to believe you are adding value and that your proposition is going to help people – all these beliefs will make a big difference to your approach.

Take as many notes as possible!

Every time you are on the phone, take notes on what your prospect is saying, because you are not going to remember everything after the call. Writing down information also helps to keep you engaged in the call, and you'll be able to remember all of the objections that were raised.

The client may say something you don't register at first. It may be a big concern to the prospect and a small concern to you. By having it in your notes to refer to later, you are in a better position to pick up on and address these concerns.

Don't underestimate the value of notes. Always keep a pen and notepad next to you when making your calls.

Top tips: Cold calling

1. **Make lists:** Who are you calling? Make sure that you group these people correctly based on their interests or industries. Calling random numbers will not help you!
2. **Script everything:** You should never just wing a call with a prospective client. Make sure that you've got a script in front of you, but don't just read it – memorise it beforehand.
3. **Know your statistics:** Track everything! You should know exactly how many people you need to call before you're able to nail down a prospect. Without this data, your job will become monotonous and soul destroying.

10

Referrals/Introductions

"People influence people. Nothing influences people more than a recommendation from a trusted friend. A trusted referral influences people more than the best broadcast message. A trusted referral is the Holy Grail of advertising."
– Mark Zuckerberg (CEO of Facebook)

Referrals are one of my favourite ways of prospecting. It's a method that I've used for years. A referral is the name and contact details of a prospective client given to you by a current client, prospect, or someone that you do business with. Referrals are very powerful. If I was to call up a referral who knew that I was going to be calling them, then that's a great opportunity.

Referrals come in many different forms so let's go through all of them to find the one that will work best for you.

The weakest type of referral is when a current client gives you the contact details of a prospect and you have to call that person to introduce yourself. You would start this call by saying: *"Hi Mr Smith. I was given your phone number by Mr Jones, who told me that you might benefit from what we do."*

A better referral would be someone's name and number from one of your existing clients, but what differs here is that your existing client would have set up the introduction for you already. An example would be your client sending an email to the referral telling them that they should expect a call from you. You would then contact that person and say: *"Hi Mr Smith. I got your contact details from my friend, Mr Jones. He said that he sent you an email. Did you receive it?"*

Taking this a step further would be when your current client sends an email to another prospect and that prospect has responded to them. You would then call up the prospect and say: *"Hi Mr Smith. My client Mr Jones sent you an email about me and I hear that you were keen to learn more?"* This sets the tone for a more positive interaction.

The next scenario would be if all of the above took place but that the prospect replies to their contact stating that they're really interested in the meeting because they need your product or service.

The best scenario of all would be when you have the contact details of the referral but they get in touch with you. An example would be if they called you up and said *"Hi Spencer. A friend of mine gave me your contact details because they told me what a great job you're doing for them and I'd like to meet with you to see what you can do for me."*

If you were to get three to five referrals from everyone that you met, you would break every sales record within your company.

It always baffles me when people say that they're unsure of how to ask for referrals, or that they "feel cheeky" asking for names and numbers of other people who may be interested in their product or service. This is beyond ridiculous. If you've done a good job with a prospect or client, then surely the least that they can do is give you a few introductions?

This is always how I conduct business. At the start of the meeting with a prospect I say, "Mr Jones, at the end of this meeting, if you're 100% happy with my service and I answer all of your questions to your complete satisfaction, can I have your word that you'll give me the details of five of your contacts who would also benefit from meeting with me?"

If you're uncomfortable with asking for referrals, then perhaps you shouldn't be in sales. This is a part of your job, and if you're doing your job well then you've **earned** those referrals fair and square!

Top tips: Advice on referrals

1. **Give your prospect a referral first:** If you're already in the sales industry, you're bound to know a lot of people. If you have a connection who might be able to help one of your prospects or clients, then put them in touch. By doing this you've more than earned the right to ask for a referral yourself.
2. **Have your clients reach out to their contact on your behalf:** Once your client agrees to give you a referral, ask them to send their contact an email that introduces you. This is so much better than you calling this person cold.

11

Email Blasts

"There is no formula for the perfect email. Authentic and honest messaging works."
– Unknown

L et's talk about email blasts. These are emails that you send out to a group of people to gauge interest. Nowadays emails have multiple filters on them so that people don't receive spam, but a decade ago when email was still a relatively new phenomenon, people would read every email sent to them.

With email marketing these days, however, unless the email is written in the right way and can get through spam filters, it's going to present you with some challenges. A personalised, well-worded email is much better than sending out bulk emails. Only 0.1% of people will respond to a mail that isn't personalised. Back in the nineties, 90% of the emails I sent were opened and 50% of these turned out to be sales leads. Sadly this has now changed, but it's still possible to get a few bites using this technique.

I'll be covering email and digital marketing later on in more detail, but if you are prospecting using email blasts, make sure that you write engaging copy and include links that are valuable to the people who you are contacting. Every single prospect will only care about what's in it for them. It's your job to engage your prospect through the email blasts, and make them feel valued, as opposed to them feeling like they're just a number. Once you have tailored this to the industry you're in, you should experience some success.

Top tips: Emailing 101

1. Send personalised emails instead of bulk emails
2. Make sure that the topic is relevant to your prospect
3. Include valuable links and information

12

Seminars and Workshops

"In any economy, there are opportunities.
The secret is knowing how and where to find them."
- Unknown

Not only are seminars and workshops great networking opportunities, but if you host your own seminars where you offer insights to a group of people, you'll be known as an expert in your field and you'll be able to convert a lot of prospects into clients. Having worked in the financial services industry for over 25 years, I've held many workshops where I've discussed growth potential in the financial markets, and this has always helped me attract new clients.

Let's think about hosting a seminar of about 100 people. Since the people attending will be in an environment where they are receiving information with no obligation, they'll be more open to talking and engaging with you because they see you as a trustworthy person. Giving people information and not expecting anything back is a very powerful tool.

Gary Vaynerchuk, who is a serial entrepreneur, did this really well when he set up a website and tried to sell wine online. In his first year he didn't make many sales, but then he started producing educational videos about wine online. People thought that viewers would watch these videos but then continue to buy their wine elsewhere, but he bet on the fact that by giving out this free educational information, people would find him trustworthy and then buy his wine. His result? Massive success!

Hosting a seminar uses a similar principle. The only difference is that it's face to face. You can speak to the group and then afterwards you can network with those people and develop business relationships. They'll trust you because you provided a safe environment where they could learn, talk to other like-minded people, and also to you.

Out of a seminar of about 100 people you'll most probably be able to convert about 50 of these individuals into meeting with you afterwards. This method might take a bit of time and organising, but if you want to experience success then you need to put in the effort.

Workshops require a person's undivided attention. And if they've taken the time to come and see you, then you're already halfway there. For an entire hour or more, these people will be paying attention to you and only you. And by the end of the workshop, you'll be the expert who they want to work with.

Top tips: The importance of presenting workshops and seminars

1. **Prospects sign up faster when they experience you in person:** Hosting a workshop or seminar on your topic of expertise is a sure way to show that you know what you're

talking about. The people attending will be able to chat to you in a comfortable and neutral environment, where they aren't pressured to buy from you immediately. Use this time to get to know potential clients, and then arrange to meet with them for a one-on-one afterwards.

2. **Give them useful information:** A nice way of being remembered after the workshop is done is to create worksheets or brochures for attendees to take home. Include your contact information and links to your website and social media channels.

13

Trade Shows

"A satisfied customer is the best business strategy of all."
- Unknown

Trade shows can be an extremely effective sales prospecting tool. They might cost some money to attend, but they're really beneficial for generating leads. Let's say, for example, that there's a bike show taking place. At that bike show, as an exhibitor you know that everyone attending is interested in bikes, or products or services associated with bikes, such as bike insurance.

If you've got a good attitude and approach, then you'll find that this is a great way of generating leads. If you haven't done a trade show before, then I'd suggest that you go to an exhibition and have a look around at the potential buyers and the potential salespeople. You'll see some exhibitors at their stands waiting for people to come and ask them questions, and then you'll find the proactive guys who are engaging with people, offering them information, answering questions, and marketing their services.

Don't just arrive at a trade show and expect attendees to stop by your stand. It's important to develop pre-show communication plans that drive people to you. There are many good tools you can leverage, from LinkedIn and Twitter, to email and direct mail. You can be creative by adding booth or show attractions, but the key is to communicate prior to the event. Then, once at the event, make sure you are friendly and welcoming to people passing by. However, don't make the mistake of pouncing on people as this might scare them away.

You'll come into contact with hundreds of people every day at a trade show, and many of these people will show genuine interest, but it's important to remember that there are other people just like you at these events, and after visiting 50 stands, it might be hard for attendees to remember who was who. For this reason, it's important to separate yourself from the crowd and offer something memorable, such as a giveaway or a competition that you can use in your post-show leverage strategy. And, whatever you do, don't forget to follow up with all the contacts and prospects that you meet!

Top tips: Making the most of trade shows

1. **Don't pounce:** While it's important to be confident and proactive in your approach, don't make the mistake of pushing people into corners or pouncing on them at trade shows.
2. **Do something different:** Make sure that your booth stands out and that you have something that separates you from the rest of the crowd.
3. **Follow up:** It's important to have a post trade show strategy in place, and to make contact with all your prospects as soon as possible.

14

How To Be Likeable

"It is not what we get, but who we become, what we contribute ...
that gives meaning to our lives."
- Tony Robbins (author, entrepreneur, philanthropist and life coach)

Sales has changed quite a lot over the years. These days, it's much more relationship driven, as is business as a whole. If people don't connect with you, trust you, and like you, it's inevitable that they'll move on to the next salesperson that they do have a connection with.

People are much more likely to do business with someone that they like, so it's important to make a good first impression, and make sure to continue to give a positive impression as your relationship progresses.

Top tips: How to be more likeable

1. **Be a good listener**: I've said it before, and I'll say it again. If you aren't a good listener, then you're going to miss crucial

things about your prospects. We listen so that we can fact find, but we also listen because it shows that you're genuinely interested in your prospect. By giving someone your full, undivided attention, you're showing that you value that person, and want to learn more about them. This makes you a lot more likeable.

2. **Be positive and optimistic**: No one likes people with a negative attitude. Positivity attracts positivity, and optimists like to spend time with other positive people, and they especially like to work with them. Given the choice of working with a negative, cynical pessimist or a positive, empowered optimist, people will always choose to do business with someone who has a can-do attitude.

3. **Be an engaging conversationalist**: It's important to be well read, well versed in cultural references, and be aware of things beyond your company, your product, and your solutions. Knowing what others like and care about allows you to converse with people about the things that they want to talk about. People are more likely to open up to you if you're interesting and able to engage in conversations.

PART III

Social Media and Sales

15

How the Internet Has Changed the Sales Landscape

"A journey of a thousand sites starts with a simple click."
- Unknown

T he world is changing. And unfortunately, if you don't keep up with the times, you are going to be left behind. The sales industry isn't what it used to be. A sales professional from the eighties wouldn't cut it today – he would be a relic.

With the internet at our fingertips, everyone is an expert, and people simply won't just accept everything they're told. It takes a lot more than reciting a few lines to win people over.

In order to be successful in what you do, you need to know your subject inside out. And if you don't, chances are you're going to be caught out. All that your client has to do is type in a basic Google search and they'll be able to tell whether or not you know what you're talking about. It's easy to spot a bluffer these days.

But the internet can also be a valuable resource for salespeople. For example, you can regularly read about all the latest trends and how they relate to your industry. By doing this, you'll be able to provide your clients with case studies and a tailor-made solution that best suits them.

You can also read the news and think about all the tactical opportunities that you could use to highlight your product or service. For example, if you're an estate agent, and you read a story in the news about the value of property increasing in your area, you could use this as a selling point. Alternatively, if you read an article that relates to your client and their business, then you could send them the link to the story. This shows that you're thinking of them, and that you're being proactive.

The internet should be used to further your knowledge, make new connections, and grow your business. Gone are the days when companies could rely solely on door knocking and cold calling. Today, people want to be able to do things on their terms and in their time.

You'll often find that if you try to call someone to talk about your products or services, they'll ask you to send them an email or the link to your website rather than talking to you on the phone. Also remember that a lot of people are proactively searching for products and services on the internet, so if you're not on those platforms then people won't see your offerings, and you'll be missing out on potential sales.

I could preach for hours about the benefits of using technology to further your business, but for the purposes of this book I've summarised some of the most important things that I've learnt about digital and social media in this chapter, that might help you on your sales journey.

Top tips: What you should be using the internet for

1. **Books:** If you want to get ahead in the business world, then you should be reading one book a week. But if, like me, you struggle to find the time to go to the book store, then just download the book that you're looking for from the web. Most books are available for download, thanks to sites like Amazon and Kindle. There are also tons of free audiobooks available.

2. **Online courses:** If you want to be taken seriously, and want to be a pro, then you'll have to have qualifications. Luckily, these days learning doesn't have to mean sitting in a lecture hall with hundreds of other students. There are many online courses available that you can do in your own time and at your own pace.

3. **Free cloud storage:** How often has it happened to you that you're on holiday and you meet someone who's interested in learning more about your business, products, or services, but you don't have the information on hand? Thanks to cloud storage services, however, you can access your information anywhere, at any time, and from any device! It also serves as a backup, so that you never lose any of your important information.

16

Is Social Media for Me?

"Think of social media as the internet.
I can't think of anyone betting against the internet."
– Gary Vaynerchuk (entrepreneur, author, speaker
and internet personality)

D o you have a business? Are you looking to grow your contact base? Do you want to be known as an expert in your field? Are you trying to make a name for yourself? Do you have something to say? Then you should be on social media! Social media is your first point of contact. After you meet someone interesting, what do you usually do? You look them up on Facebook or LinkedIn. If you hear about a business or corporation, where do you go to learn more about them? You would go to their website or their social media pages, of course.

Think of your social media pages as an extension of yourself. Essentially they are the gateway to you, who you are, and how others perceive you. I've met so many interesting people, developed business relationships, and sold more stuff than you can imagine, all by using social media.

They call it a social networking tool for a reason! Use it to network and connect with people, and you'll soon have more contacts and prospects than you could ever dream of.

I recently met a man who was very proud of the fact that he wasn't on social media. I understand that some people view these platforms as a distraction, but I don't believe that you should be living your life under a rock either. Being on social media doesn't mean incessantly checking your notifications or spending hours scrolling through your news feed. If you control the time you spend on social media, then it won't control you.

Many companies block social media platforms so that their employees can't mess around on them during work hours. Although I'm not a believer in using social media for social purposes when you're at the office, using it to connect with prospects, as well as using it to keep up with all the current news and happenings, is very beneficial.

Adding your social media details on your business cards and CV is the fastest way for people to get to know you and get in touch. And as a salesperson, since one of the biggest challenges that we face is people trusting us, shouldn't we be making it easier for all of our prospects and clients to familiarise themselves with who we are, what we do, and how we can help them?

Another thing that's very important to potential clients is being available to them when they need us. Once again, social media makes that much easier. Perhaps some people wouldn't agree with me that it's important to always be reachable, but these days things don't happen only between 9 a.m. and 5 p.m.

If you shut down at 5 p.m. and if you're only reachable on your office line, then you're going to lose a lot of business. Be smart about your business strategy, and make sure that you're available to the people who need you.

17

Social Media for Business

"Social media is about the people! Not about your business. Provide for the people and the people will provide for you."
– Matt Goulart (founder of Ignite Digital)

I t always baffles me when I chat to companies who don't believe in investing their time, resources, or money in social media. They'll spend hundreds of thousands of dollars on billboards and television adverts, and yet they're not prepared to spend a fraction of that on digital marketing. In today's world, it's imperative to have a social media strategy in place.

Contrary to what some people believe, social media is much more than just a way to get noticed online. It allows you the opportunity to grow your brand, connect with your current customers, and generate real leads for your business. And what's even better is that social media lead generation is actually very cost effective. There probably isn't a more powerful sales tool on the internet than social media. Sites like Facebook, Twitter, LinkedIn, and Instagram can become effective and profitable sales tools.

Social media networks are incredible and affordable resources for businesses looking to promote their brands online. Obviously everyone's aim for social media is to achieve a lot of engagement, but the changes to Facebook's algorithms have made it increasingly difficult to get organic reach. And so if you're not reaching the numbers you want, it won't break the bank to boost your posts and pages with paid advertising options. In this way, you can reach new audiences and grow a significant following in a short amount of time on a small budget. That's why I use a mix of organic and paid-for content.

It's important that you choose and nurture the social platforms that work best for your business, so that you don't spread yourself too thin. A lot of small businesses tend to join every single social media platform that there is, without knowing how to use them properly first. My advice would be that you choose your social media platforms carefully. For example, if you're in financial services, then your main social network shouldn't be Instagram, which is a very visual platform; it should rather be LinkedIn. LinkedIn lets you connect with other industry people, share thought leadership articles and infographics, and provides the opportunity to establish yourself as a leader in your field.

If, however, you were selling services or products that lent themselves to visuals, then Instagram, Pinterest, and Facebook are for you. I'm not saying that you can't be on all of the social media platforms, but you do need to know which platforms would suit you and your target audience best, and where your content would receive the most engagement. If you want to create a successful social media strategy, you should familiarise yourself with how each social network operates, the kinds of audiences you can reach on that platform, and how your business can best use each social network.

Let's talk about Facebook for a minute. Facebook is the biggest social network on the web. With nearly 1.8 billion active users, Facebook is a great medium for connecting with people from all over the world.

Whether you're an individual, or have your own business, when people search for you online, your Facebook profile will pop up. Since this is a platform that most people are familiar with, they're bound to click on this first, which means that the information that you supply on your Facebook page has to be relevant.

You could lose many sales and prospects if your Facebook page is full of irrelevant posts and outdated information. Have a clear description of who you are, what you offer, and how people can reach you. And then make sure that the content you post is both engaging and informative. These days anyone can create content, and if you want to be seen as an expert in your field, then you should be uploading videos, using the Facebook Live tool, and sharing your knowledge.

Facebook also lets you target your audience according to a number of variables, such as interests, age, gender, income, geographical region, or occupation. Targeting potential customers in this way means that cold calling people who may not be interested in your product or service is potentially a thing of the past. The customisation options are virtually limitless, allowing you to maximise every cent you spend. Pay-per-click advertising (PPC) is extremely powerful, and if you're not already implementing it into your sales strategy, you should be! Pay per click, also known as cost per click, is an internet advertising model used to direct traffic to websites, where you pay when the ad is clicked.

But before you can really maximise a social media advertising strategy, you'll first need to create a following, and in order to create a following, you'll need to have content that is engaging, relevant, and interesting. Think about what you have to say, and how you're going to say it.

A lot of people employ other companies to do their social media, but if you're going to develop your brand, then you need to make sure that the brand is you. This means being very hands on and involved in everything that is posted.

Digital advertising has without a doubt changed the entire marketing, advertising and sales landscape. For example, whereas billboards used to be a very popular way of getting people's attention, these days passengers are too busy looking at their phones to pay attention to billboards. So you should focus on reaching your audience where they usually are – on their phones. Smart businesspeople take advantage of the popularity of social media, and if you're good at it, you'll generate great leads.

If you do a Facebook Live, Instagram Live, or a Periscope session once a week, where you speak about your products and services and offer people advice, you'll slowly build up a following. This creates online traffic, which in turn generates contacts and leads.

Another way to create a following is by uploading videos to YouTube. These videos should highlight your expertise in your field in order to build credibility and position you as an industry leader. People will start thinking of you as the go-to person in your sector. You can put your details on these social media platforms for people to call you directly, or you can send them to a portal where they input their details and you contact them. Think of every way possible that you can introduce yourself, your products and your services on social media. If you do it the right way and you're committed to it fully, you'll see fantastic results. But if you do any of these methods half-heartedly, then they won't work.

Top tips: Getting started with social media

1. **Ask questions:** Ask your audience questions that are

relevant to the product or service that you sell. This will work as research for you, and your audience will also be more interested in engaging with your content.

2. **Do your homework:** Spend time learning about social media and how it can help your business. It's more effective than cold calling and door knocking. There are so many different platforms and options for what you can do, so spend some time exploring and discovering everything available to you.

3. **Know your audience:** Make sure that you are very familiar with your target market, and that you tailor your content to suit what they are interested in.

18

How To Engage with Prospects Using Digital and Social Media

"Quit counting fans, followers and blog subscribers like bottle caps. Think, instead, about what you're hoping to achieve with and through that community that actually cares about what you're doing."
– Amber Naslund (author)

You may be familiar with the phrase, "Content is king". And for today's fast-paced, digitally savvy world, it certainly is. There are so many people producing content these days – from videos to articles to images – that if you want to stand out from the crowd and make people stop for a minute and listen to what you've got to say, you'd better make sure that your message is worth their time.

I make a point of producing original posts, videos, and blogs on a daily basis and then posting them across all of my social media channels. I give my audience all this expert information for free, only wanting one thing in return – for people to take note of what I'm saying and use my advice to help them on their business and sales journey.

When engaging with prospects on social media, you must also

remember that people tend to be rather sceptical about what they don't know. Very few people trust what they haven't experienced or learnt more about. It's kind of like buying a car. You wouldn't purchase a new vehicle without first test driving it, would you? For example, I've got an online sales university called Make-It-Happen University, where I teach people how to sell. I can't expect people to pay for my courses before they first experience who I am, what I do, and what the university offers.

When people visit your social media pages, they're essentially window shopping – they're checking you out and looking at your specs. If you manage to intrigue them, or capture their attention, you're much more likely to turn these 'window shoppers' into serious buyers.

This is why it's also important to have all your product information and click throughs available on your social media pages. You should make it as easy as possible for people to find out what they need to know about you. If they don't find what they're looking for, then they'll leave your page and follow someone else.

Infographics, visual content, and videos are far more likely to grab someone's attention than a boring, text-only post. And original content performs far better than an outdated article that you found on the web that's already been shared one million times. Think about what your target market would be interested in, and then give them more of that content.

Ask questions, get to know your followers, and offer helpful solutions. If you talk *at* someone, then they won't engage with your content. However, if you talk *to* them, and let them know that their opinions matter to you, then they'll be more likely to stick around and comment on your posts more often. And that's what you want on social media – engagement. The more people who like and comment on your posts, the more people will see your content, and the more followers you'll attract. If no one ever engages with your content, then Facebook will mark you as irrelevant, and you'll have a pretty hard job of breaking through the rest of the clutter on social media.

Top tip: Use insights to break through the clutter

1. **Regularly look at your Facebook insights:** Know your audience demographics, such as their gender, age, and location. Having this knowledge is very important. For example, if you know that your following is predominantly male, then you can focus on addressing more males in the videos you produce, or you can offer exclusive deals just for your male followers. Knowing your statistics is always important!

19

Ever heard of ClickFunnels?

"Selling is like pouring water down a leaky funnel. You guide water into the top of funnel, but the only useful water is that which reaches the spout."
- Unknown

ClickFunnels is a service, developed by online marketing extraordinaire Russell Brunson and his team, which is essentially all about building different types of marketing funnels. A sales funnel is a series of pages your visitors go through to reach a certain goal.

ClickFunnels are also really important if you want to make money by selling your products and services online. With online sales, most people set up a website to try and sell their products. However, you won't make a lot of money by doing this if all you have is a flat website. Using ClickFunnels will help you generate more leads and ultimately make more sales.

With ClickFunnels, visitors will go through a lead magnet, where you'll be able to gather their contact information, so that you can follow up with them via email. You'll then have a sales page created to sell your product. This first sales page can be an eBook, or something similar, that you sell for about $10. If visitors purchase this, you can then upsell them on your other products that are usually more expensive, such as access to your online course. This is what's known as a sales funnel, where you convert visitors to your website into paying customers.

Every salesperson needs a sales funnel. Whether you're selling houses, cars, a book, or even financial services, using sales funnels will help you attract the right clientele to grow your business. But it's important to note that not all sales funnels are the same. There are different results and outcomes with each kind of sales funnel, so it's essential to know which one works for you and your business.

The first thing that you'll need to do when creating a successful sales funnel is to identify the problem that your potential customers have. This is a problem that your customers can't solve themselves. This could be as simple as them not knowing how to start a new business, being ignorant about how to use social media, or not knowing how to prospect for new potential clients.

The next thing that you'll have to do is provide a solution to their problem. How can your product or service help them? For example, your product could be an eBook that gives them ten helpful tips to start their own business. Or perhaps your service or product could be an online platform that teaches them all about social media. In order to do this well, you'll need to be skilled in your subject matter.

The last step in creating an effective sales funnel is to keep up to date with all the latest technology and digital tools and trends. As I've mentioned before, the world is changing, and you can't just say that you don't understand how digital technology works. If you don't know, then educate yourself.

A sales funnel will only be as successful as you are, so you've got to be committed to be the best, and give people what they really need and want. Your skills will attract people to your sales funnel, and will keep them engaged and interested in what you have to offer.

Top tips: Sales funnels and getting people interested

1. **How to attract traffic into your sales funnel:** A good way of attracting traffic is to have a blog. A lot of businesses have great success with sending Facebook ad traffic to their blogs, and then retargeting the people who visited the blog to an opt-in page. Once these people opt in, you then move to the middle of your funnel, where you will start to build trust and authority, usually through email marketing, phone sales, or webinars.

2. **What to do after trust is built:** Once you have attained people's trust and authority, you'll be able to get your prospects to buy your introductory offer. After that you can then sell them your main core offer. You'll be able to house all of this content on ClickFunnels. I've seen many entrepreneurs and businesspeople grow their revenue significantly by doing this.

20

Email Marketing Vs Social Media

"The incredible brand awareness and bottom-line profits achievable through social media marketing require hustle, heart, sincerity, constant engagement, long-term commitment, and most of all, artful and strategic storytelling."
- Gary Vaynerchuk (entrepreneur, author, speaker and internet personality)

L et's talk about email blasts. These are emails that you send out to a group of people to gauge interest. Back in the nineties when email was still a new phenomenon, people would read every email sent to them, so email blasts were a lot more effective. These days, however, people are a lot more selective about the emails they read. In addition, email inboxes have filters, so bulk emails often end up in the spam folder.

How things stand currently with email marketing is that unless the email is written in the right way and can get through spam filters, it's going to present you with some challenges. A personalised, well-worded email is much better than sending out bulk emails. Only 0.1% of people will respond to a mail that isn't personalised. As I've mentioned before, back in the nineties, I had a 90% open rate for emails being sent out and an engagement rate of 50%. Sadly this has changed, but it's still possible to get some bites using this technique.

If you are prospecting using email marketing, make sure that you write engaging text and include links that are valuable to the people you are emailing. Every single prospect will only think about what's in it for them. It's your job to engage your prospect through the email blasts. Once you have tailored this to the industry you're in, you should experience some success.

Top tips: Making the most of email marketing

1. **Use short and punchy subject lines:** The longer the headline, the lower the opening rate. Keep it short and to the point!

2. **Define your audience:** Make sure that the content that you're sending out is relevant to your audience. For example, if you were selling cosmetics, then you should be targeting women. If you're sending out communication about lipsticks to men, your numbers will be terrible. Know who your audience is, how old they are, what their interests are and what they respond to.

3. **Encourage subscribers to follow you on social media:** Once a person opts in or subscribes to receive emails from you, you should send them an email in your auto responder that asks them to connect with you on social media. Not only is this a great way of growing your social media following, but they'll also be able to see more of your content and offers.

4. **Use the 80/20 rule:** If you use email purely to push your product, then people are going to opt out or unsubscribe. Make sure that you're adding value to them 80% of the time – with relevant information, blog posts, podcasts and videos – and then you can push your products or services very subtly for the other 20%.

PART IV

Goal Planning

21

What Is Goal Planning?

"Setting goals is the first step in turning the invisible into the visible."
– Tony Robbins (author, entrepreneur, philanthropist and life coach)

If you want to achieve success in your life, you need to know exactly what you want. One of the most powerful things I learnt early on in my career was how to set clear and definite goals. I knew what I needed to do each day and I got those things done. Without goals, we have no direction.

I remember when I was first introduced to the concept of goals at the age of 20. My boss gave me a sales target and said that if I hit it, I'd get an upgraded company car. I had my target that I had to reach in a set period of time, and I was incredibly fired up about hitting it. I was fully committed, and I broke the goal down and worked out what I needed to do each and every week to achieve it. It was a fundamental lesson that has stayed with me ever since.

For the past 26 years I've set new goals for myself annually, and I work towards achieving them in a very structured manner. Every year I have a financial goal, a 'feel-good' goal, and a health goal that I want to reach. I revisit these goals every day so that I can stay on top of them. I'm incredibly thorough and I break down my goals into the finest detail possible. What I find that also helps a great deal is analysing weekly statistics. I can't stress enough how important these numbers are if you want to achieve any goal. Keep statistics on everything you do!

When did you last set a goal for yourself? And how committed were you to achieving it? Very often, people think of goals the same way that they think about aspirations. But if in your mind you're grouping your goals with the things that you'd *like* to achieve, instead of the things that you *need* to achieve, you're never going to reach your goals in a timely manner. That's why it's so important to be specific about the goals that you set.

It's also essential to give yourself a set amount of time within which you aim to achieve your goals. Don't overwhelm yourself by listing too many goals in too short a time frame. I've coached a lot of people who tend to stress themselves out by writing down hundreds of goals at once. This isn't the correct strategy.

When setting your goals, it's important to tackle one thing at a time. Set a timeline in which you aim to achieve these things by and stick to it. When you know that you're working on a deadline, you tend to get things done faster.

There's a proverb that states: "Where there is no vision, the people perish," and that statement could not be more appropriate for this chapter. Without vision, you won't be able to see where you're going. Without goals, you won't have anything to look forward to and to motivate you to keep on going. Setting goals for yourself means that you know where you are headed. Without focus and goals you'll just drift along, and you'll never know your true potential.

Top tips: Questions to ask yourself to help you set goals

1. **Where am I now?** In order to know where you're going, it's vital to be realistic about where you stand currently.
2. **Where do I want to get to?** When you think of your life in five to ten years' time, where do you see yourself? It's important to know what you want for your future self. Do you want to work your way up to a managerial position at your company? Or do you want to start your own business? Be specific!
3. **How am I going to get there?** It's essential to visualise yourself getting to where you want to be, but you have to be realistic as well. Think about the things that are going to help you achieve your goals.
4. **What's holding me back?** Make sure that you note down everything that's keeping you from currently achieving your goals, and then deal with them head on.

22

Turning Your Goals into a Science

"A goal without a plan is just a wish"
- Antoine de Saint-Exupéry (French writer, poet, aristocrat, journalist, and pioneering aviator)

How can you score if you don't have a goal? So many people want to be successful, but unless you're clear about what you want to achieve and you know exactly what you've got to do, then you're not going to get anywhere. Goal planning should be a core aspect of any professional's life.

Think about what you want to achieve. Is this something that you *want* to achieve or something that you *need* to achieve? A need (or a must) is far more powerful than a desire (or a want). The first thing you should do is focus on what your need is. Let's say for example you need to earn $100,000 by the end of the year. You have 12 months to achieve this goal. How are you going to go about this?

Turn this into a science by taking your goal amount and dividing it into 12 months. This will give you a monthly target. In this case that would be around $8,340. Then break the month down into four weeks to get your weekly target ($2,085). You can then work out your average commission per sale. If your average commission per sale was $695, then you'll know that you have to achieve three sales per week to reach that target. That can be your starting point. Then you'll need to know how many prospects you'll have to meet weekly in order to make one sale.

Breaking your goals down into bite-sized chunks makes them far more achievable. If you stick to this, and do what you need to do every single day, then you'll get to where you need to be. By doing it this way, you'll probably find that you'll land up exceeding the original goal that you had.

Tony Robbins talks about a massive action plan. You have to put huge amounts of effort and energy into every activity. Create a plan and then action that plan. Make sure that you've done everything that you can to make your plan succeed. By doing it this way, even if you fail, you know that you gave it your all. Goals require a timeline and a target. Talk yourself into everything that you do, stay focused, and be clear on your targets. If you take one goal at a time, you'll be more effective.

Top tips: Setting targets and using timelines

1. **Be specific:** Before setting a timeline, you must define your goal. Be as specific as you can be. For example, don't say that you "want to make more money". Write down exactly how much money you want to make and when you want to make it by.
2. **Break your goal into manageable pieces:** We often look at the sheer magnitude of our goals and get overwhelmed. Break your goals into sub-goals. For example, if like me your

goal is to write a book on your subject of expertise, then simply take it one chapter at a time, or even one page at a time.

3. **Avoid procrastination:** One of the biggest problems that people encounter when trying to reach certain targets is the issue of procrastination. Even the most dedicated and disciplined person can sometimes fall prey to procrastination. This is why it's important to remind yourself of your goals and targets on a daily basis, so that you can stay on track.

23

Stay Away from Negative People

"You can't live a positive life if you have a negative mind."
- Unknown

I speak about the effect that negative people can have on a person quite a bit in this book. Negativity effects morale, performance, motivation, and energy. You must have heard the saying, "You are the company that you keep". The more you hang around people who tell you that something can't be done, the more you'll begin to believe them. If you want to stay focused, and be buzzed and excited about life and your career, then you need to surround yourself with the right people.

Successful people tend to hang around other successful people, and positive people attract other positive people. Be with individuals who are hardworking, motivated, and optimistic. This goes for all areas in your life, professional and private.

I've consulted many companies battling with staff turnover and productivity issues over the years, and the common denominator has always been a negative individual who seems to affect the entire office morale and company culture. All that it takes is one person's negativity to destroy a great environment. These people thrive off gossip, scandal, and negativity, and it's their aim to get as many people into their corner as they can. My suggestion to each and every company that has a person like this is to get rid of them immediately. I have no tolerance for this kind of behaviour, especially because negativity breeds more negativity. Nothing positive can grow in a stagnant, unconstructive environment. The businesses that have taken my advice on this have come back saying that, after letting the negative person go, they have seen their other employees' productivity increase, and noted a positive shift in attitudes throughout the office.

Perhaps that's why I have no time for office banter and water cooler talk. If you're at work, then you are there to do a job. And, if you have your head screwed on right and have all your goals in check, you won't have time to sit around drinking coffee and discussing pointless things.

Another obstacle that can prevent you from achieving your goals is laziness. This has got to be my absolute pet peeve. There is absolutely no excuse for laziness. You can't expect to be a millionaire if you're not prepared to put the hard work in, and you definitely can't be a successful salesperson if you're not prepared to put in the hours. If you have a goal, then stick to it. Map it out, and then commit.

Often, laziness is disguised. I once had an employee who used every excuse in the book to cover up his own laziness: *"It's not possible"*, *"I would do it, but it's never been done before"*, *"We're not getting the right results because people just aren't interested"*, *"It's not me, it's the product!"*. I can't tell you how much it frustrates me when people tell me that something can't be done! Obviously this employee didn't last long in my company. I replaced him with someone who enjoyed being challenged, who was excited about going where no one had gone before, and who never gave up when he faced a difficulty. It's individuals like these who will always go far in life. Their positivity is infectious, their work attitude is admirable, and their ability to stay focused on achieving their goals is unwavering. If everyone was more like this, then we would all experience huge success, and we'd have many more millionaires in the world!

If you're reading this and you have a negative person in your life who is affecting your happiness and success, then cut them out! Conversely, if you happen to be the negative one, then commit to being more positive. Do things for others without expecting anything in return, be thankful for the things that you have, and appreciate the people around you. Changing your behaviour will see you achieving things that you never thought were possible. When you have a negative attitude, you'll miss so many opportunities that could have come your way. But when you're positive, you are more open to accepting good things. You'll be more energised, more motivated, and ready for huge success!

Top tips: Banish negative thoughts

1. **Take responsibility:** Many negative people tend to play the victim. They blame other people or external factors for their lack of success. By taking responsibility for what you've done wrong, you're able to put it behind you and start again, this time in a more positive manner.
2. **Help someone:** Doing good deeds doesn't just make you look like a good person; they make you feel like a good person. And, when you feel good, invariably you'll be a lot more positive.
3. **Be grateful:** List everything that you have to be grateful for, even if all that you're grateful for is the fact that you have a roof over your head and a job. Each day try to find more things that you're thankful for, and you'll see the list grow.
4. **Exercise:** Exercise helps everything. It'll boost your morale, it'll help keep your goals clear, and it'll keep you motivated. Trust me!

24

Eat, Sleep, Drink, and Think Work!

"A dream doesn't become reality through magic; it takes sweat, determination, and hard work."
– Colin Powell (American statesman and a retired four-star general in the United States Army)

I coach a lot of people who have struggles with their business and achieving their goals. The business problems that they have genuinely come down to: *"I can't get the results I'm looking for"*, *"I can't get the number of clients I need"*, or *"I'm struggling to hit my targets and achieve my initial goal."* Invariably, nine times out of ten, you'll find that the common denominator with these people is that they're not prepared to put the hard work in, or put in as much hard work that's actually needed in order to achieve their goals.

If you want to build a prosperous business, be a successful salesperson, or simply reach the goals that you set for yourself, then you're going to have to understand that this requires an enormous amount of hard work. And let's be clear – an enormous amount of work doesn't just mean starting an hour earlier every day. An enormous amount of work requires sacrifice. This means that you won't be able to go home and watch television after work, and that you can't take weekends off to relax. In order to be successful in today's business world, you're going to have to commit your life to eating, sleeping, drinking, and thinking work.

Also, avoid the trap of thinking that you can relax when you experience your first bout of success. Real success won't have staying power unless you do. The trick to my prosperity over the years has been that every time I achieved a goal, I was even more committed to working harder to achieve my other goals. I've always wanted to be the best, and if you want to stay on top then you've got to keep ahead of your competition at all times. Perhaps this is also why I wake up at 4:30 a.m. every morning. While other people are sleeping, I'm making things happen. And the more I accomplish, the more I want to accomplish.

With this intense work schedule, some people might raise the issue of burnout. Let's get one thing straight – it's not work that leads to burnout, it's doing things that you don't love. That's why it's important to be passionate about what you do. If you enjoy what you do, then work won't always feel like work, and you won't mind putting in those extra hours.

Some of you might think that it is not realistic or possible to work more than is expected of you, but if you really want to be successful, then luxuries like holidays and resting should be secondary to you. Those things will come later, but right now what do you want more - to laze around on a beach doing nothing, or to be the next Grant Cardone, Gary Vaynerchuk, or Tony Robbins?

When I commit to a new project, I'm prepared to work morning, noon, and night, seven days a week. Most people take more holidays in a year than I've taken in five years. But I don't miss holidays, because I'm committed to my craft and I'm getting my finances to where I want them to be, so that I can live life on my terms. And even though not everything should be about the money, it is an incredibly liberating feeling to be able to not have to worry about such things. You too can get to this point – if you're prepared to work for it.

If you only want to work from nine until five, five days a week, then you're not going to get to where you want to be, and you're not going to achieve the goals that you've set for yourself. If you truly want success, then you've got to be dedicated, motivated, persistent, and, above all else, incredibly hard working!

Top tips: How to motivate yourself to work harder

1. **Form habits:** As some people tend to struggle with staying motivated at all times, it'll ultimately be easier to form habits. This could be waking up an hour earlier every day, or starting your work week on a Sunday so that you can get a good head start on your week.
2. **No pain, no gain**: Hard work is not easy, but it is worth it. If you want to be better, then you're going to have to venture outside of your comfort zone.
3. **Reward yourself:** Reward your hard work and commitment with something small every time you achieve a goal or hit a specific target. This could be anything from a watch you've had your eye on, to a fancy dinner with a loved one.

25

The Six Steps to Smart Goal Planning

"If you aim at nothing, you will hit it every time."
– Zig Ziglar (author, salesman, and motivational speaker)

In order to keep momentum that will drive you forward in achieving your goals, you'll have to think S.M.A.R.T! This means that the goals you set will have to be Specific, Measurable, Achievable, Relevant and Timely.

Before you start mapping out your goals, it's important that you commit. You'll have to make a deal with yourself that you'll commit 100% to everything that you write down. This means giving it your all, and not backing down no matter how tough things get. Here are the six steps that I follow when setting goals:

Step one: Commit completely

If you're not 100% committed from the very beginning, then you might as well give up before you even start. How badly do you want to be better? How much do you want to succeed?

Step two: Understand why

If you want to make a positive change in your life, then you need to understand why goals are essential. It's also imperative to recognise why these goals are important to you. You need to know exactly what's involved and where you want to go.

Step three: Create goals

Now that you're committed, and you understand why it's important to set goals for yourself, it's time to set your actual goals. As I mentioned before, I group my goals into financial goals, feel-good goals, and health goals.

When setting your goals, it's also important to list all the people who can help you. Who, apart from yourself, can hold you accountable? And who will support you in achieving your goals? Who will your goals ultimately affect? It's essential to know these things.

Step four: Break your goals down into tasks

As I mentioned above, it can be quite daunting and overwhelming to achieve a goal if you don't break it down into manageable chunks first. Write a to-do list every single day, and make sure that you get these tasks done. The path to achieving a goal often involves ticking smaller tasks off, one at a time.

Setting daily tasks for yourself makes your goal actionable. This means that you're not just simply setting a goal, but you're taking action every single day in order to achieve your goal.

Step five: Devise a schedule

It's vital to commit to a schedule. If you don't, then you'll be going nowhere slowly. Be specific about when you want to work on your goal and when you want to achieve it. If for example, you want to go on an expensive Christmas holiday, then you can't start working on your goal only in November. Be realistic, and know what time works best for you.

Step six: Assess and reassess

The reason why it's important to revisit your goals on a daily basis is so that you can assess whether or not they're still important to you. If they are, then assessing and reassessing them will help you stay focused and motivated. You'll be able to assign new tasks and activities for yourself, and you'll keep moving forward towards your vision and your goals.

PART V

Four Gears to the Sales Process

26

The Sales Process

"Sales success comes after you stretch yourself past your limits on a daily basis"
- Omar Periu (Businessman and motivational speaker)

I'll never forget my first sale. I was living in Thailand at the time and went to see a man called Mr Goodey, who was the CEO of a big company. Being only 23 years old, I was terrified, but I went in, spoke to him, and followed my sales process. He told me to send him a proposal and come back and see him in a couple of days. He also told me that when I came back to see him, we'd have lunch together. I was thrilled, to say the least!

When I went back, he became a client on the smallest investment possible, but the fact that he'd signed with me made me feel great nonetheless. We didn't end up leaving the office for lunch like I had thought we would, but celebrated with cup-a-soups instead!

I'll never forget my first client. He knew that I was young and inexperienced, but he gave me a chance. That day was a turning point for me, and after that my sales skills went from strength to strength.

There are thousands of sales methodologies and theories out there that may or may not work, but after years of doing this I have mapped out four simple gears for the sales process that will ensure you always experience success. Although every person is different, the salespeople who I've coached always experience a better success rate when they go into the sale with four easy-to-remember action points. During this chapter, I will break down the sales process into these four steps, namely:

1. Rapport
2. The introduction
3. Fact-finding
4. Closing

Prior to meeting a prospective client for the first time, you need to have practised and rehearsed your sales process. This will ensure that when you finally meet them face-to-face, you'll be aware of the process that you have to go through and the meeting will go more smoothly. You're also more likely to get subsequent buy-in from your prospect. In addition to the above four steps, it's also important to remember the following rules when meeting your prospect face-to-face for the first time:

Rule Number 1: Make sure that you look the part. We've spoken about the importance of appearance and good personal hygiene in previous chapters, but I can't stress this enough!

Rule Number 2: Properly introduce yourself with a firm handshake. When you meet your prospect, it's important that you engage with them immediately. Make sure that your eyes are wide open, and that you have a smile on your face. This may seem very basic, but you'll find that when you do this, the person will be more responsive. Remember that the prospect is not interested in you, they are there for themselves, so don't get sucked into talking about yourself and monopolising the conversation. The meeting should revolve around *them*!

Before you can move through the sales process, there are key questions you need to ask in order to get the prospect's buy-in. Make sure that you engage in conversations led by open-ended questions.

As I mentioned in Chapter One, open-ended questions are questions that the prospect has to answer with anything other than "yes" or "no". They include questions like who, what, where, when, and why.

Open-ended questions allow you the opportunity to learn a lot about your new prospect, which will not only help you secure this deal with them, but you'll be able to log these details for your future dealings with this client and secure further deals. It is absolutely essential that you make a great first impression and that your prospect likes you and thinks of you as a credible person or business contact from the very first meeting.

It's normal for prospects to be a bit suspicious of your intentions when they meet you for the first time. I've often heard the line: *"You're just trying to sell me something"*. Put your prospect at ease and break through their barriers by asking them questions. This doesn't mean, however, that you should overstep the mark and talk about subjects that you shouldn't be focusing on too soon, such as very personal issues. Remember to start by building rapport and putting them at ease with the following rules for conversations: Work – Social – Family (I'll go into more detail about this later).

During this chapter, I'll walk you through the four gears to the sales process. Apply these learnings and you'll sail through your sales meetings.

Top tips: Why asking open-ended questions is necessary

1. **You can collect more detail:** If you don't ask, then you'll

never know. Asking your prospect open-ended questions gives them the opportunity to share things with you that they wouldn't normally volunteer otherwise.

2. **You'll get an inside look into how they think:** Every person likes to feel that their opinions are unique. Giving them the opportunity to share their thinking with you will help you to understand them better and will also make them feel as though you're genuinely interested in them.

27

Gear One: Building Rapport

"Rapport is the ability to enter someone else's world, to make him feel that you understand him, that you have a strong bond."
– Tony Robbins (author, entrepreneur, philanthropist, and life coach)

Never underestimate the importance of building rapport. Rapport is essentially the ability to relate to others in a way that creates trust. And when it comes to building relationships with prospective clients, trust is vital. Building rapport with a prospect makes them feel comfortable and open to future suggestions.

When building rapport, it's important to understand what's involved. It's about settling the prospect so that they're calm. It's also an opportunity for you to learn about your prospect and better understand who they are, what they do, why they do it, and what's important to them.

Building rapport is essentially about asking open-ended questions. If the questions you're asking get a "yes" or a "no" response, then you're not learning anything of importance about your prospect, and you won't be able to understand what they need or want.

Great questions are vital to knowing your prospect well. If you didn't know that your prospect had children, for example, then you wouldn't be able to sell them an education savings programme. Conversely, this prospect is very unlikely to buy a two-door sports car from you.

As mentioned previously in Chapter One, you can break down rapport building into three areas. The first area is work, the second area is social, and the third area is family. Work is where we ask open-ended questions about their job. Examples would be:

- *"So Mrs Jones, how long have you worked here?"*
- *"What is your role in this company?"*
- *"What would you say are your strengths and weaknesses?"*
- *"What exactly is it that your company does?"*

Listen to what your prospect says and remember it so that you can use this information later. Once you understand why they do what they do, ask them questions about their social life.

"So, Mrs Jones, what do you do when you're not working?" Perhaps they have an interest or a hobby. Let's assume that the prospect enjoys playing golf when they're not working. *"How often do you play golf?", "Who do you play golf with?"* Once again, remember their answers.

After you have asked about work and social you can move onto the next subject, which is family. *"Can I ask how big your family is?", "How long have you been married?", "Tell me a bit more about your kids. How old are they?" "Where do they go to school and why did you choose that school?"*

By asking these questions you'll get a good understanding of their decision-making process. If your find out that their son is at a good school, for example, then perhaps they are hoping to further his education at a university. You can then use this to your advantage.

Spend about five minutes on each topic. If the prospect tells you that they have two daughters, don't then start talking extensively about your own children. Keep the conversation about them.

Once you've managed to get your prospect to a place where you know more about them, you then need to get to the point where you are able to understand the psychology and the dynamic at hand. The prospect may be thinking a few things at this point. They may be thinking, "*This guy is trying to sell me things that I don't want*", or "*I don't have much time. I hope he's really quick*", or "*I hope I'm not obliged to buy something. I'm not sure I can trust this person.*" These feelings are absolutely natural. But if you're not aware of what's going on in your prospect's mind, then you'll most likely bulldoze your way through the sales process without taking a step back to consider their thoughts or concerns.

It's really important that you take care to understand the psychology and the dynamic that exists between the prospect and the salesperson. If you get it right, it's going to be great. If you get it wrong, it's going to be a problem, so make sure that you're sensitive to that.

Remember that the fact that they're meeting you means that there's an interest. It's your job to take them from the small amount of interest that they may have, to convincing them that you're the right person for them. Your goal is to get them over those barriers and hurdles so that they are confident that you're the individual they should be dealing with when it comes to your area of expertise.

You've got to increase their level of trust. You've got to pull their barriers down and take away their fears. Then you'll be in a much better place as you move through the sales process. However, while it's important to establish rapport and ask questions, it's also important not to overstep your mark and ask questions that come across as too intrusive, even if they are work related. Finding the right balance will ensure that your prospect feels comfortable with you and is happy to share information with you.

Top tips: Building rapport

1. **Body language:** Adopt a similar stance to your prospect. Mirroring them might make them feel more at ease.
2. **Be interested:** Take a genuine interest in what your prospect has to say. Smile at them and make them feel important.
3. **Keep it about them:** Don't go off topic. Remember to always bring the conversation back to them, and keep asking them open-ended questions.

28

Gear Two: The Introduction

"Show value, create an experience,
and always strive to exceed customers' expectations."
– Shep Hyken (customer service expert, author, and speaker)

L et's talk about introducing the client to your business. If you've completed gear one of the sales process correctly (building rapport by asking open-ended questions), then it means that up until this point your prospect has been doing most of the talking. This is important because it allows you to learn vital information. In the second gear of the sales process, however, it's essential that you have time to speak as well.

You will need to introduce your company, explain what you do, how you work, what your credentials are, and how you are going to add some value to your prospect. It's important that you lay down the terms of business so that you can engage in the right way.

A good way to start is by saying something like, *"Let me tell you about my company, and how we work. Then we can see if there are any areas of synergy".*

The first thing that you should discuss is your company – for example, how long it's been in business, and also how long you've been working there. Tell your prospect about your areas of expertise, as well as the things that you don't do so that there is no confusion. For example, if you're an estate agent who doesn't handle mortgages or something similar, it's important that they know this.

You can then tell them about the products and services that you offer. After you've shared all of this, then talk about your own work experience briefly, for example, *"I've been in this industry for ten years and I've had the following successes…"* Make sure that your prospect knows that you're an expert in your field.

At this stage, your prospect may not know what they want to buy, but be assured that they're there because they have an interest. Once you've explained how your company works and told them a bit about yourself, it's important that the client knows what the terms of business are. We call these the rules of engagement.

If, for example, you were in financial sales, you could say the following:

"Mrs Jones, the first thing that I'm going to do today is complete a fact-find that's going to enable me to understand your current financial situation. I'm going to ask you questions such as how much money you make, how much you've saved, what kind of investments you've made, what real-estate you have, and what assets and debts you have. Once I've established all of this, then I will flag the areas that I think you need to work on. If you agree with me, then I'll do the homework for you and together we can devise something that will meet your requirements. It's then my job to go to the market place and find that product that will match your needs, which will take me a bit of time. I will, however, do this for you on one condition. Quite simply, if I do all this work for you and you are happy with my proposed solutions, then we can go ahead and do some business. So what I'm trying to say here is that I don't want to waste your time and I don't want to waste mine. If we establish today that you have a need, I can design something with you that will address this need. I will then go to the market to find that solution for you. When you're 100% satisfied

with what I've done and the product solves that problem for you, we can go ahead and do some business together and you can become my client."

By doing the above, you've clearly spoken about the current situation and made sure that the client understands the terms of business. People will often want to know about charges at this point, but don't get sucked into explaining charges until you know exactly what they want and have done your research.

It's also important to let your prospect know that, if they feel that you have added value, then you'll be asking them for introductions to other like-minded people at the end of your meeting. It's imperative to have this engagement and get the buy-in of your prospect. By doing it this way, they agree upfront that they owe you a few introductions if they're happy with you and your services.

Top tips: Introducing yourself and your services

1. **Keep it simple:** Time is valuable. Your prospect isn't interested in hearing you ramble on about yourself for an hour or two, so you'll need to be as succinct as possible. Tell your prospect a bit about yourself, what you do, and what services you offer, but don't let this part of the process monopolise your whole meeting.

2. **Make sure that they're aware of your terms of business:** If you want to get ahead in the sales game, then you have to ask for introductions. Make sure that your prospect is aware of the fact that you'll be asking them for names and numbers after your meeting.

29

Gear Three: Fact-Finding

"The art and science of asking questions is the source of all knowledge."
- Thomas Berger (novelist)

Once you've built rapport, helped your prospect to relax, got to know them a bit better, and introduced your offerings, you can then move onto the next gear of the sales process, which is fact finding.

We've already established the importance of asking questions, whatever you happen to be selling. It's crucial to do a fact find with everyone you meet. Your questions should enable you to understand the current situation that your prospect is in. Think about it this way – if you were to go to the doctor, he or she would ask you about your symptoms, in order to give you the best treatment. Fact-finding is essential, no matter what business you're in! Be sure that you understand the answers that you're given and ask further questions if necessary so that you're absolutely clear.

Let's talk about selling your prospect financial services. If you're talking to them about their children and their education, it's important to understand whether or not university is a priority for them. Some people want their children to go to university, but for others this isn't essential. Ask the correct questions so that you can understand your prospect's thinking. If their child is currently going to a school that is a fee-paying school, then I would assume that the parent is keen on paying for a good education for their child. I would ask the following questions:

- *"What school did you choose for your daughter to go to?"*
- *"Why did you choose that school?"*
- *"Tell me more about the type of school it is?"*
- *"What kind of fees do you pay at that school?"*
- *"Since you're sending your child to a fee-paying school, are you hoping to send your child to university?"*
- *"Which university would you like to send her to?"*

If it were life insurance that I was talking about to my prospect, then I'd ask questions such as:

- *"What kind of allowances or preparations have you made to make sure that your spouse has enough money should something happen to you?"*
- *"What plans have you got in place to make sure that your family is protected?"*

These kinds of questions are good fact-finding questions. We can establish where our prospect is and where they'd like to be. Some people might have thought about the future, but some people haven't. There is no point in guessing. Rather ask questions and learn. Probe until you find a need in your prospect. It's important that we ask great questions, learn as much as we can, and gather this information so that we can get ourselves into the next gear of the sale. If we haven't asked the right questions, then we haven't established the need, and if we haven't established the need, then what are we going to sell?

The problem may not always be apparent to the prospect, so the only way to get them to understand where they are is to ask open-ended questions. Then it's your job to find a solution to their problem.

"Mrs Jones, I see you don't have life insurance. Why is that? Why have you chosen not to protect your family?"

You've got to get a good bank of information and turn that information into something tangible in terms of a problem and then come up with a solution to that problem. But don't share the solution with your prospect too soon – they need to come to a decision by themselves first. Hopefully they'll realise at this point that they need your help and should buy your product.

Let's use life insurance as an example again. You know that your prospect's problem is that they don't have life insurance, but how do you fix this? You simply tell your prospect that you're going to ask them some more questions so that you know what type of product they're looking for. Once you have an idea of what they need, then you can go out to the market and find the right product or solution for them.

Obviously when it comes to life insurance, there are a lot of products out there, so it's important to find the right solution to suit your prospect's needs. You'll need to know what term they want the insurance to be over (five years, twenty years, etc.), what currency they would like the premium to be paid in, how they would like to pay their monthly contributions and lastly, how much life cover they think they'll need. Do not, however, confuse need with want; if you're selling life insurance, you'll have to calculate how much they actually need.

Get confirmation from your prospect that if you find the product that they're looking for, then they will buy it from you and become your client. You can't do research like this unless you have commitment from their side, so here you need to go into the trial closing. This is to ensure that you don't waste your time. *"Mrs Jones, can I just be clear that if I can find a solution for you that satisfies all of your needs, then we will sign a contract the next time I see you?"*

The prospect will most likely say yes, but if they don't then you can't just carry on. You need to stop and ask them if you've missed something. If your prospect doesn't want to commit to anything at this point, then you have to go back to the drawing board because you obviously haven't created a solution that addresses their need. You've probably created a solution for a "would like". Don't confuse these two things. When someone needs something it's non-negotiable – they must have it!

If your prospect has agreed to your terms, then you've got to get a few things done before the meeting ends. Firstly, you've got to book a second appointment with them that is within the next two to three days. The sooner you meet with them the better, as the information needs to be fresh in their minds. The next step would be to make sure that your prospect is clear on what is expected of them in the next meeting – that is, you will present a solution and they will sign on and agree to become to be your client. Be very clear on what you want as your payment; if you're after referrals or introductions, then this is the time to discuss it.

The idea of completing the fact-find is to identify the areas where the prospect needs to do some work. There will be different areas that you can look at during the fact-find if you are an insurance broker or a financial adviser. If you're doing a retirement plan for your client, then you'll need to give them a financial calculation. *"So, Mrs Smith, currently you're earning $50,000 a year. When you get to retirement in 20 years' time, how much do you think you'll need as an income?"*

Your prospect may think that they don't need as much money as they're currently earning when they're retired, but they'd be wrong.

When people get to retirement age at 65, they'll most likely still have a good 20 years ahead of them, and they'll want to do the things that they never had the chance to do when they were working. People therefore need at *least* as much as they were living on prior to retirement when they retire.

Once you have both agreed on the amount of money your prospect will require to live on per year, you will then need to do a calculation to show them how much they'll have to save in order to achieve that goal. Create some urgency with your prospect. Every month that they delay will push the premium up. If they want to start saving as soon as possible, then it's time for you to do some design work with them. This means that it's back to asking questions.

These questions would be: *"Would you like to save monthly, quarterly, or yearly?"* Then you could ask, *"Would you like the freedom to stop this plan at any time and pick it up again later, should you lose your job?"* *"Would you like the freedom to be able to make ad-hoc contributions, should you receive a bonus?"*

The next questions you would ask are around their risk and reward: *"What kind of risk exposure do you want for your money?"*, *"Based on this risk, what kind of return would you be looking for?"* Then you'll move on to ask about charges: *"How much do you think is a reasonable amount for you to pay per year for this product?"* You've also got to ask them other questions about who their beneficiary would be, should they die before retirement age.

When you're in the sales process there are some things that you'll need to memorise for your fact-finding exercise. These questions differ according to what you are selling. For example, a house and a car are tangible products, that is, physical objects. Financial services and insurance, however, are intangible and so can only be perceived indirectly. You will need different types of questions for the different products or services you are selling. A question for a tangible product such as a car could be: *"What are the top things you'd love to see in your new vehicle?"*. A question for something intangible such as a retirement plan could be: *"How much money per month do you think you can retire comfortably on?"*

Top tip: The best questions to memorise for the sales process

The best questions revolve around wanting to know about the prospect's current circumstances so that you can help them with their future situation. Here are three examples of questions to memorise the next time you're doing a fact-find:

1. *"Why is this product important to you?"*
2. *"Have you ever owned something like this product before?"*
3. *"What do you like or dislike about your current product and what more are you hoping to get from a similar product?"*

30

Gear Four: How To Close

"Sales are contingent upon the attitude
of the salesman, not the attitude of the prospect."
– William Clement Stone (businessman, philanthropist, and author)

The final stage of the sales process, gear four, is your closing. Once you have the perfect product or service for your prospect, and they are satisfied with it, then it's time to close. But before you do the work and can close, go in with a trial close. *"So, Mrs Smith, if I can find a product that can do all of these things, are you happy to go ahead and do some business with me?"* If at this point, she's still not entirely convinced, then you need to go back and find out what's missing. Do not proceed if your prospect says "maybe", "probably" or "I hope so". The goal here is to elicit a confirmation or commitment. You can only move on to closing if you get a "yes".

After confirming that your prospect is happy, you can then set up another meeting with them within the next two or three days. Your prospect should have agreed that if you find a solution for them, they will become your client. Let them know what documents they'll need to bring along with them, for example a copy of their passport, bank statements, medical information, bank account details, etc.

Before the end of this meeting, ask your prospect whether you have added value to them and their situation. If the prospect says "yes", then ask them if they think the value you added could be beneficial to other people who they might know. *"You mentioned that you play golf with your friend John. Do you think he'd be interested in any of my services?"* Push to get four or five introductions. By doing this, you'll be able to avoid all the hassles of cold calling.

Now let's focus on your second meeting with your prospect. Make sure that you have a very positive attitude and are dressed appropriately. At the start of the meeting, you'll have to build some rapport again by asking more questions, so that your prospect is settled. Thank them for the introductions that they gave you at your last meeting and tell them whether you've had any successes with these introductions.

You've done your homework and are now able to present a tailor-made solution for your prospect's needs. Once you have gone through everything with them in detail and they are aware of all the costs, ask them if they have any questions. At this stage, you're likely to get one or two questions. Avoid seeing these questions as objections. Nine times out of ten, if you have done your job correctly, then these questions won't be real objections.

If you've met your prospect's need and you've made sure that they can afford the product, then it should be an easy sales process. Write down all of their queries, and then ask your prospect if they will sign the contract after you've answered all of their questions to their satisfaction. If they agree, then take it one query at a time. When you have addressed all their questions, ask for a copy of their documents so that you can complete the paperwork.

Once you have finished the administration work and contract, express how much you're looking forward to working with this person as a client and finding them solutions that meet their needs. Arrange another time to see them once the premiums have gone through. A deal is only a deal once you get paid.

If you're a salesperson, then you'll know how important it is to master the art of closing. You put a lot of time, effort, and money into generating leads. If you only manage to close one in five leads, then that's a lot of time, effort, and money wasted. Your prospect has also taken time to meet with you, so if you don't manage to close, then they might begin to negatively perceive the business that you're in, or the products that you're selling.

There is a cost to everyone involved if you don't manage to close. It will affect you, your company, and your prospective client. It's your duty to get your prospect over the line, and your duty to make that sale. As an employee, you have to close the leads that you've been given. Make sure that you master the art of closing!

Top tips: Making 100% sure that the deal is done

1. Clients still need to say "yes", and you still need to get a commitment in writing. The process is only completed when you've got the signed paperwork and they've made payment. Don't let your guard down too early if these things haven't happened yet.
2. Test for commitment throughout the sales process. Make sure that your prospect is really interested and that this is a product or service that can truly help them.

31

Some Examples of Closings

"A-B-C. Always be closing."
- Blake (character in the film *Glengarry Glen Ross*)

A lways have an arsenal of closings that you can remember and use. It typically takes five closings to get a prospect over the finish line, but most salespeople only remember four (and invariably they won't make the sale because of this). It's imperative to have different options that you can use as closing techniques. The more closings you memorise, the higher your chances are of making the sale.

If a prospect gives you an objection that you don't know how to handle, you won't close the deal. If you can't handle objections in the moment, then it's because it's not instinctive. As a salesperson, you should know your closings as well as you know your alphabet. When your prospect gives you objections, you should be able to address them without thinking twice.

Sit down

When you're in a negotiating and closing situation, always make sure that both you and your client are sitting down. It's also important to sit beside your prospect if you can. When you're sitting down, you can engage with each other, and you can go through the process of negotiating without anyone feeling uncomfortable. In this situation, your prospect will also be unable to walk away.

Use humour and innovative approaches

Using humour is a great way to ensure that you close your deal, as people are more likely to make decisions when they're more relaxed. While you're going through the paperwork with your future client, share some stories that might lighten the mood a bit. If they are going to be spending money, then they'll want this to be a good experience. However, be sure to steer clear of humour that involves politics, religion or anything offensive. For example, I once sent a giant cookie to a prospect with a hand-written card saying, "Mr Prospect, I would really like to take a bite out of your business, but until such a time that I do, please enjoy this cookie". The prospect found this to be a funny, innovative, and unique approach and he contacted me immediately so we could do some business together. Appealing to a prospect's emotions will often result in a positive outcome.

Don't take no for an answer

The difference between a good salesperson and a great salesperson is that when faced with an objection from a prospect, a great salesperson won't give up and will ask again. They don't let it go and will say something along the lines of: *"Mrs Smith, we've spent a lot of time with one another and I know that we're not over the line yet, but can I get just ten more minutes of your time so that we can go through this again? I promise that it'll be worth it".*

A lot of salespeople will give up when they can't get their prospect over the finish line. But you'll often find that if you ask one more time, you will be able to close the deal. Remember that your prospect has invested their time already – they've done their research online, and they've come to meet with you. This means that they want to do business with you; they just need to find the correct way of doing it. If you give up after the first objection, then everyone's time is wasted and nobody wins.

Don't leave your prospect alone

The moment you leave your prospective client's side is the moment that you lose control of their thoughts. There may be situations when you leave them temporarily in order to fetch paperwork, or to ask your boss a question – such as the possibility of a discount for this prospect – but I would encourage you to remain seated with them until you've closed the deal. If you need something, send a text message, but never leave their side! Control their thoughts and the situation by walking your prospect through the sales process and staying with them.

Top tips: Common mistakes made with closings

1. **Not greeting people properly**: Make sure you always greet people appropriately. You should shake your prospect's hand firmly and have a big smile on your face.
2. **Misinterpreting their fears**: It's your job to understand exactly what their fears are and why they have them.
3. **Not being optimistic about challenges**: See every problem as an opportunity.
4. **Selling someone with a "no"**: Never tell someone "no" and never tell someone to wait. Always remember that people are on tight schedules and they want to deal with someone who treats them like a priority.
5. **Giving your prospect numbers until you know exactly what they want:** Avoid mentioning figures and data until you're sure of their needs; it's just going to confuse them.
6. **Telling your prospect "I don't know"**: Make sure that you know your subject well enough so that you always have an answer. You need to be an expert in your field.
7. **Not giving your prospect hope**: They want to be reassured that they can get their situation resolved.

PART VI

Skills for Success

32

Success

"If you want to go big, stop thinking small!"
- Unknown

I've met so many people in the sales industry who, after experiencing just a little bit of success, assume that they know everything there is to know about sales and have nothing left to learn. Let me assure you – no matter how long you've been in the game, there is always something that you can learn and there are always ways to better yourself. If you want to be taken seriously, and want to be seen as an expert in your field, then you'll have to be prepared to put in the hard work and be open to the fact that there are other ideas and learnings out there that can help boost your performance. Personally, I make a point of trying to learn something new every day, even if it's something small.

If you've purchased this book, then you're obviously interested in learning more about sales, and I commend you on taking the necessary steps to bettering yourself and furthering your personal and professional development. As most great salespeople would know, the first step to becoming a better salesperson is taking the time you need to invest in yourself and in your future.

My parents have said to me that, from a young age, I would often tell them I'd be a millionaire one day. But I know that I wouldn't have been able to achieve that dream and get to where I am today by taking short-cuts. In life, there are no quick fixes. You either put in the hard work, or you don't. But don't expect to find success if you don't have the necessary skills. In this chapter, I'll be discussing exactly what you'll need in order to get ahead in life and in business.

33

Be an Expert

"The true entrepreneur is a doer – not a dreamer."
– Nolan Bushnell (American electrical engineer and businessman)

I n order to make it as a successful sales professional, or any other kind of professional, it's imperative that you're an expert at what you do. This will require time and a great deal of effort, but most people can become experts in their field if they really want to. All that's standing in the way of you achieving this is your drive and your desire to succeed. If you want to earn the respect of your clients and colleagues, then it's time to get serious about your career.

Education is the gift that keeps on giving. There is no such thing as being "over-qualified". If, however, you don't have the time, money, or resources to pursue full-time degrees or diplomas, then there are plenty of online courses available – you can sign up for mine at http://www.makeithappen.university/. You'll be able to do these courses in your own time, and can learn at your own pace.

In Chapter Three we discussed the benefits of the internet and digital media. Technology has changed the sales game and has enabled us to have the answer to just about anything at our fingertips. Who are your competitors? What are they doing online? What products and services do they offer? How do their products differ from yours? What are they doing differently? How can you boost your own sales by learning from them? Asking yourself these questions and researching the answers on a daily basis will ensure that you have a competitive edge and that your clients will always receive the most relevant and up-to-date advice or information.

Imagine how unprofessional you would look if you were presenting a product that you hadn't done enough research on to a prospect. If your prospect were to ask you about how your product compares to others on the market, and you weren't familiar with all of your competitors, then you'd lose your credibility and that sale. Likewise, if you don't know enough about your subject matter in general, there is no way that you'll be taken seriously. Aim to be the person who has all the answers!

Books are an incredible resource for any businessperson. They're affordable, and also make for great conversation starters. I make a point of reading at least one book a week, and if I'm stuck for time then I'll listen to an audiobook in the car between meetings. It's easy to get stuck in a rut or a certain way of thinking. Listening and learning from fellow experts will open up your mind to all sorts of ideas and possibilities that you may have not considered yourself.

At the start of my career, I was working in London and it took me an hour to get to the office every day. I used this time to listen to audiobooks by motivational speakers and legendary sales experts such as Zig Zigar and Brian Tracy. Then later, in my twenties, Tony Robbins came out with "Get the Edge", which was a six-CD personal-coaching programme. I can't tell you how much his CDs would motivate me. I listened to them on the way to work, between meetings, and on the way back home from work. This time in the car became my time for professional development and training. It was at this point in my career that I started making a lot of money, and these CDs were instrumental in helping me to push myself. I'm still a huge fan of Tony Robbins because of this and I make a point of going to his training seminars as often as possible.

If you want to experience success, then you have to realise that every single minute of your day is valuable, and you could be doing something to better yourself instead of listening to rubbish on the radio. Keep your mind stimulated at all times!

Top tips: How to become an expert

1. **Be a builder:** No matter what your field, you need to see yourself as a builder. Think of your ideas, products, or services as your materials; you are building something that directly affects people. And, just like a house, you need the correct foundation. Make sure that you work carefully and precisely. Take time to learn your craft.
2. **Be present:** If you want to be an expert, then you'll need an incredible amount of focus and concentration. Dedicate at least two hours at a time to developing your skills. During this time, you'll need to be completely present (this means no distractions!). Once an action becomes automatic, you'll be able to observe yourself and analyse your own strengths and weaknesses. If this is difficult for you, then ask others to observe you so that they can critique your behaviour.
3. **It takes time:** When mastering a new skill, or becoming an expert in your chosen field, you'll have to sacrifice a great deal of time. There will be times when you'll want to give up, but what separates a master from a student is that the master trusts the process and never gives up. Practise makes perfect.

34

Reflecting and Self-Coaching

"We cannot become what we want by remaining what we are."
– Max Depree (American businessman and writer)

How often do you take the time to critically assess yourself and the things that you do? Great salespeople should engage in self-coaching or advanced learning all the time. Get into the habit of reflecting, either at the end of every sales meeting, or at the end of every day.

After every meeting with a prospect or client, ask yourself questions about how the meeting went. Be honest with yourself. Possible questions could include:

- *Did I meet all of my objectives in that meeting? If not, what could I have done differently to achieve them?*
- *If I were my prospect, would I be happy with the service that I received?*
- *Could I have been better prepared for the meeting?*
- *What was the best part of the meeting?*
- *Were my strengths evident?*
- *Would my prospect recommend me to their friends, family, or colleagues?*

- *What did I learn from this meeting?*
- *Have I taken the necessary steps in order to move the relationship forward in a positive way?*

Critically assessing yourself in this manner will do wonders for your development. It'll help motivate you to be better, and will drastically help your sales process. I've always had a winning mentality – I delve into this later on in the book – but in order to win, you'll have to take a long, hard look at yourself. If you want to be the best, you'll have to get rid of all your bad habits, and the only way to do this is by critically assessing yourself on a daily basis.

Constructive criticism is a good thing. When I was a youngster, my boss asked me what middle-aged senior executive would trust me, a 23-year-old kid, with their life savings. Looking at it in this way made me realise that if I wanted to be taken seriously, I would have to put in the work. My boss gave me a box full of financial services books and every night I was tasked to go home and read them.

I studied these books for months, until I knew the subject better than anyone else did. It was only then that I realised that my prospective clients were slowly starting to have faith in my knowledge. It felt really good that people trusted me because I had become an expert in what I was selling. Don't forget that trust, just like expertise, is earned.

The only person responsible for your development and growth is you! Do courses, go to seminars, find a mentor, and make a concerted effort to keep nurturing your mind. When you stop doing these things and you become complacent, your development will stagnate, as will your credibility.

Group training sessions are also very beneficial. Once a week, get together with three or four of your colleagues and roleplay with them.

Go through your sales process and at the end ask your colleagues to critique your performance. Although it may not be easy to hear criticism, your colleagues will be able to pick up on any strange quirks you may have and will be able to advise you on how to present yourself and your services better. Doing exercises like this will also help you to think on your feet. Preparing for client objections is a big part of the sales game, so make sure that you know how to master this.

Top tips: How to get the most out of self reflection

1. **Don't be too negative:** Being too hard on yourself might kill your confidence, but the right amount of self-criticism will help heighten your performance. For example, you should focus on critiquing your behaviour rather than your personal attributes. Instead of thinking that you're not intelligent enough, rather look at the reasons why you're not achieving your full potential. For example, you may be spending too much time in front of the TV, instead of reading self-help books or doing online courses.

2. **Think of the things that you could do better:** Once again, this doesn't mean analysing all of the things that you think you *can't* do. Instead, think of any opportunities that you may have missed, and then make a commitment to pursue them. Start small and then build your way up.

3. **Ask questions:** Pretend that you're not critiquing your own work. Then write down a list of questions you might have on this work. Possible questions could include: *"Have you given this task your all?"*, *"How do you plan on taking this further?"*, and *"Do you believe that you've done everything possible?"*. Once you've got a list of these questions, answer them as honestly as you can.

35

Jack-Of-All-Trades, Master of None

"The jack-of-all-trades seldom is good at any.
Concentrate all of your efforts on one definite chief aim."
- Napoleon Hill (author)

We're all familiar with the figure of speech used in reference to a person who has many skills but no sole focus. You'll find that there are an increasing number of 'Jacks' these days, but bear in mind the value that people place on true expertise. For example, if you were sick, you wouldn't choose to see someone who had flunked out of medical school. You would only want to see a qualified doctor.

While it is possible to be knowledgeable in more than one subject, it's important to master one thing at a time. Take time honing your craft. Read everything that you can get your hands on that deals with your subject of expertise. Then, once you've mastered one subject, you can move onto the next.

I often get questions from people who want instant gratification in their business endeavours. These people, who have hardly invested any time in their business, want to experience overnight success, and if they don't, then they move onto something else.

You can't expect to build an empire in a day. Great things take time. It took me ten years to get to where I wanted to be professionally. Ten years of working my way up the ladder, improving my skillset, and pushing myself to my limits.

So many people call themselves 'entrepreneurs' these days, but more often than not, these are just people who want to have as many different revenue streams as possible, without having to put too much work in. Let me just assure you that this strategy will never work.

Build one thing at a time. Make sure that you're giving your business idea the attention that it deserves, and then once it's a success, you can move on to getting involved in other things. The relationship that you have with your business should be similar to the one that a parent has with his or her child. You wouldn't just leave your newborn to fend for herself, would you? You would have to feed this baby, nurture her, care for her, and be there to watch her grow. The same applies to your career.

Top tips: How to master your craft

1. **Choose learning instead of earning:** If I've learnt anything over the years, it's that you shouldn't just be driven by money. When faced with two opportunities, you should always go for the one where you will learn more. A lot of young sales professionals or entrepreneurs might be tempted to go for the higher-paying job, but it is important to also consider other aspects that come with this job. If one of the

opportunities comes with mentorship, training, and learning, then you should go for that one. If you grow your mind and your skillset, then you will undoubtedly grow your wallet down the line as well.

2. **Accept that failure is inevitable:** If you want to become a master in your field, then you have to realise that you are bound to make mistakes. Try out as many new ideas as you can. Some will fail, but others will succeed. If you're afraid of failure, then you'll ultimately be afraid to take any risks. And if you're not taking risks with your business, then you'll never become a massive success.

3. **Find a mentor:** If you want to be the best, then you have to learn from the best. With the right mentor, you'll be able to streamline your work process and get expert advice on how to grow your business.

36

The Five-Hour Rule

"Never stop learning, because life never stops teaching."
- Unknown

Oprah Winfrey, Bill Gates, Warren Buffett, and Mark Zuckerberg all have one thing in common. Despite being extremely busy, throughout the duration of their careers they've all set aside at least an hour a day, or five hours a week, for activities that could be classified as deliberate practise or learning. This phenomenon is now also referred to as the five-hour rule.

The five-hour rule can be grouped into three different segments: reading, reflection, and experimentation. These five hours are outside of your normal work routine and require complete dedication and concentration. Most professionals in the workplace tend to focus on productivity and efficiency, instead of focusing on improvement. But with the five-hour rule, you set definitive targets to improve yourself and your expertise. As a result, just five hours of deliberate learning a week can set you apart from everyone else.

Many people measure how successful their day was based on how much they get done. Once again, the focus is on productivity instead of on improvement. People who embrace the five-hour-rule are the ones who aren't in a race, but ultimately end up achieving more in the long run.

The only person who you're competing with is the person you were yesterday. By committing to being a lifelong learner, you commit to bettering yourself and your work. Step outside your normal routine and challenge yourself daily. For me it always comes down to goal setting. Where do you see yourself in one year from now? Five years from now? What will you be doing ten years from now? And what do you want to learn in the time between now and then?

Top tips: How to get started with the five-hour rule

1. **Read one book a week:** Bill Gates reportedly reads 50 books a year, Mark Zuckerberg reads at least one book every two weeks, and Elon Musk grew up reading two books a day. Reading will not only help you learn new things, but it'll also help test your understanding.
2. **Map out what you want to learn:** Without goals, you will have no direction. But instead of just having goals for the things you want to accomplish, you should also have goals for the things you want to learn.
3. **Set aside time for deliberate learning:** Take classes, go to workshops, participate in conversations, observe others, and take time to reflect. All of these activities will help you considerably, so make sure you create space in your day for them.

37

Winning

"Winners never quit and quitters never learn."
- Vince Lombardi (American football player, coach, and executive in the National Football League.)

Achieving the things you want will come a lot easier if you adopt a winning mentality. Winning isn't everything – it's the only thing. As much as I'd like to take credit for those words, they were said by the late Vince Lombardi. I also had this piece of advice printed on my very first business card: *"Life's battles don't always go to the stronger or faster man. But sooner or later, the man who wins is the man who thinks he can."*

Whenever I'm asked how I've been so successful over the years, my answer is that I like to win and I never settle for second place. When I set my mind on something, there's nothing that can stand in my way.

This can-do attitude has seen me achieve things that many didn't think were possible. A few years ago, when I broke my back, I was told that I would no longer be able to do the sporting activities that I enjoyed so much. I had always been a very active person, so this injury was standing in the way of me doing what I loved. Instead of feeling sorry for myself and listening to any negativity, I set a goal for myself and I managed to get through that tough period. I'm now stronger and fitter than I've ever been in my life.

I've never been a quitter, and once I set my mind on achieving something, there's nothing that can stop me from reaching that goal. Everest had always been on my bucket list, and after overcoming my injury, the thought of pushing myself to my physical limits was really intriguing. And so, much to the dismay of my wife and parents, who were worried about the dangers of Everest, I decided that I would climb it. In June 2017, I achieved one of my lifetime fitness goals when I summited past Everest Base Camp to Kala Patthar, which is 5,700 metres above sea level.

Climbing Everest was much tougher than I thought it would be, and if I didn't have my positive mindset or a winning mentality, I would never have been able to get through it. Imagine climbing up a neverending flight of stairs for eight to nine hours a day for nine days straight. Then imagine the oxygen getting less and less as you journey higher and higher. Experiencing that altitude and the lack of oxygen is something that you can never quite prepare yourself for, so invariably your body takes a bit of a beating. Sleep will become challenging, you will be sore and fatigued, and on top of all of this you'll go days without showering or experiencing any sort of warmth or comfort. Climbing that mountain was without a doubt the toughest thing I've ever done in my life. That being said, however, I'd do it again in a heartbeat.

On the day that we landed in Kathmandu to start our summit, I remember feeling super confident. I had trained and was ready for anything. The first day of walking was quite easy, and I think that made me believe that I'd been cheated a little bit, because I then started to wonder if the rest of the trip would be a walk in the park. But of course, this was a false sense of security, as the next few days saw me experiencing some of the most intense physical exertion of my life.

Every day we would wake up at about 5:30 a.m. have some breakfast, and then start walking at about 07:00 a.m. On average, we'd walk for about eight hours per day. Some days we experienced very steep climbs with very little reprieve, and other days we walked through dusty paths with rocks everywhere.

The nights were cold, dark, and quiet, but this allowed me time to reflect. I thought about my family, my life, the good and bad experiences, and issues that I'd perhaps been making bigger than they actually were. When you're up there, pushing yourself to your limits, the things that you once thought were so important suddenly don't feel important at all.

In those dark and trying times, it was always my mind that got me through. I kept on telling myself that "I can", and "I will". Whether you're working towards a fitness goal, a personal goal, or a business goal, be conscious of where your mind wanders; if it wanders to a place of self-doubt or negativity, stop it in its tracks. A winning mind is a positive mind. And a positive mind will see you achieving anything that you want to achieve. Then, once you've successfully ticked that goal off your list, move on to the next thing you want to conquer.

The way you think affects all aspects of your life. Learn to listen to that voice inside your head and recognise how your thought patterns affect your decision-making process and how you handle stressful situations. Having a positive mental attitude is vital. Negative thoughts don't get you anywhere.

Straight after my Everest adventure I cycled 1,070 kilometres from

London to Geneva to raise money for children with special needs. It rained almost every day, I was freezing cold, and I suffered from terrible tendonitis, but did I give up? Not a chance! Even though the rain made it impossible to enjoy the scenery, I kept my eye on the prize and maintained my focus.

Negativity holds you back and keeps you from achieving the things that you are more than capable of achieving. The secret is an unshakeable belief in yourself and your abilities. Make a point of verbalising all of your positives and write down all of your success stories. Achieving a winning, positive attitude can be incredibly effective in your quest for success.

Set yourself a goal of doing something that scares you every year. This should be something that pushes you, motivates you, and challenges you. But in terms of professional development, I would say that you need to do something new every month. Keep on pushing, and keep on winning!

At the end of the day, winners never quit and quitters never win. And the people who believe in themselves the most are the ones who are going to make it happen!

***

Top tips: How to build a winning mentality

1. **Visualise everything:** Whether you're running a race, or giving an important pitch, it's imperative to visualise yourself achieving your goal. See yourself running, picture yourself crossing that finish line, and imagine what you would feel in that moment. Experiencing these things in your mind before you experience them in reality will help to prepare you for the challenge ahead.

2. **Tell yourself that you're a winner:** Mindset is everything. If you don't believe that you're the best, then how can you expect to be the best? A journalist once asked me to describe myself. I told her that I'm a winner. Some might consider this thinking a bit arrogant, but how else are you going to boost your confidence? Believe in yourself wholeheartedly!

3. **Prepare for the win:** While it's important to believe that you're a winner, you'll also have to put in the hard work. Research has shown that with 10,000 hours of practice, you can become a pro at just about anything.

38

Have a Great Attitude

"If you think you can or you think you cannot, you are probably right!"
- Henry Ford (founder of the Ford Motor Company)

Have you ever met a successful person who didn't believe in themselves? I sure haven't. That's because winners have a quiet confidence – occasionally bordering on arrogance – that gives them enormous self-belief, enabling them to perform at a high level.

This kind of confidence is a skill that comes from disciplined practise. You have to learn how to quieten the voices of doubt in your head that tell you that you can't win. I always make a point of having a great attitude. It annoys me when someone tells me that something can't be done. No matter how impossible you think something is, you should always say that you're going to find a way to do it. If it's never been done before, then aim to be the first person to do it. When a person says, "I can't", this is just making excuses.

I've had many people come up with many excuses over the years, but I firmly believe that, if we can put someone on the moon, then anything is possible. Negative people are like a poison to an office. Confident and positive people are never defeated. They keep persisting in the belief that their best is good enough to prevail in the end.

The biggest problem that I see people making in the sales industry is that they don't have a good enough attitude. Before you even think about starting with your sales process, your attitude has to be spot on. If your prospect doesn't believe that you love what you do and what you sell, then they're not going to be interested in buying from you or being your client.

People prefer to buy from people who have a great attitude. If someone makes you feel good, there's a decent chance that you will buy from them. A can't-do attitude will lead to a negative experience for your customer. But if you're warm, welcoming, and optimistic, then that will set the tone for a productive and positive encounter.

If you knew that you were losing out on sales because of your attitude, would you change it? The most important person you have to sell to is yourself. You have to sell yourself on you: your package, your service, your skillset, and your deliverables. You must believe in yourself and that what you are doing is helping people. Complaining and pointing fingers will only work against you.

You need to think about how you feed your mind and how you respond to things. Replace all the negativity in your life with positivity. Focus on your career and your future. Remind yourself that you have a duty to your spouse, your colleagues, and to your employer. Take responsibility for your success! Fine-tune your attitude, make sure that you're organised, and then follow that up with focused action.

How to verbally deliver a good attitude

Communicate positively with a can-do attitude. Focus on saying things like, *"Yes sir!"*, *"No problem at all, I can definitely do that!"*, *"I'm very keen to do that!"*, *"That's an easy thing for me to fix!"*, etc. Be the guy or girl who can!

You and your attitude are the difference between you and your competitors. If most people are being negative, your can-do attitude will stand out and people will buy into that. Verbalise that you are the kind of person who people will want to do business with.

Top tips: How to maintain a great attitude

1. **Dress like a winner:** Every day, dress like you're going to meet the biggest prospect of your life.
2. **Look happy:** Light up with a big smile when you meet people. Be approachable, warm, engaging, and dynamic.
3. **Have service in your heart:** Be focused on servicing your clients. Always find them the best possible solutions, take care of them, and let them know that you care. If they feel you care, they will buy into you.
4. **Be genuine:** Many people will notice if you are being genuine. Always be honest and stay humble!
5. **Write down a gratitude list:** Think about all the things you are grateful for. This list refreshes your mind and reminds you that you are in a good place!
6. **Exercise:** Keeping active not only boosts your energy levels, but it also boosts positivity. Ever wondered why athletes get so grumpy when they don't get enough exercise? It's because they rely on the endorphins that they get from exercising to keep them motivated.

39

Know Your Competition

"You can't look at the competition and say you're going to do it better. You have to look at the competition and say you're going to do it differently."
– Steve Jobs (American entrepreneur, business magnate, inventor, industrial designer, and co-founder of Apple Inc.)

Competition is good for you

There are a lot of debates out there about whether or not competition is a good thing. Some say that you should just put your head down, work hard, and focus on what you're doing, rather than what your competitor is doing. But let's be honest – if you weren't competitive by nature, then you wouldn't be working in sales!

While you shouldn't necessarily be comparing yourself to others all the time, if you do away with healthy competition, you'll be robbing your-self of the opportunity for growth. It's important to be able to bench-mark yourself against your peers. I've always been fuelled by my competitors; they keep me thinking and moving forward. Competition takes us out of our comfort zone and forces us to better ourselves and find innovative ways to sell our products and services.

If you aren't constantly working on yourself, then you're not innovating, and if you're not being innovative, then you've lost your competitive edge. The failure to innovate leads to obsolescence. As I said earlier in this chapter, it's vital that you commit to your personal development.

In addition to competing with yourself, however, you should be competing with others as well. This doesn't necessarily mean nasty competition, but rather learning from people in an attempt to better yourself.

Competition is the very essence of a sales professional's existence. Study it. Embrace it. Love it. Use it as a motivator to fuel you. Use it to take you to the top of your mental game. Develop an unstoppable, competitive mindset, and you'll sell yourself to success.

Top tips: Why competition is good for you

1. **It forces you to be more creative:** If you happen to have a lot of competitors in your market, then you'll know that innovation is key. In order for your product or service to stand out, you'll have to think outside the box.
2. **It teaches you:** In life, there is ultimately always a winner and a loser. It's inevitable that sometimes your competition will come out on top, and you'll lose. It's up to you how you let this affect you. If you take it as a learning opportunity, then your competition will be helping you grow. Chances are you'll be all riled up and you'll want to prove that you're not a loser, so you'll work even harder the next time round. And next time

you just might win! I've failed many times, but I always choose to see these detours as positives instead of negatives.

3. **It forces you to take chances:** Once again, if everyone did the same thing, no one would stand out and life would be utterly boring. Having competition will force you to make choices that you may not have made before. Always trust your gut!

4. **It helps you achieve your goals:** if no one else was performing, and everyone just earned the same amount of money for merely showing up at work, then there would be no need to push yourself to be better. I was motivated by success, a great lifestyle, and a secure future, and you don't get those things by sitting on the couch. You have to be the best! And if you want to be the best, then you'll need to compete with the best.

5. **It makes life more exciting:** One of the best feelings in my life was when I won an award for being the best sales professional. I had been competing with another man for the title and had put in more effort than you can even imagine. But when I won, it was all worth it. Competition and 'winning' give you a thrill that you wouldn't otherwise be able to experience.

Know your competitors

In addition to knowing what your biggest competitors are up to, you should make a point of setting some time aside every day to find out who the new players are in your industry. Find out what they're doing and how you can do it better.

Appreciate your competition. Learn from them. Use them to amplify your motivation and enhance your competitive mindset.

Always make sure that you're one step ahead. What you've got to realise is that there are other guys out there who are hungry for your clients' business. If your eyes aren't open, then you could risk losing what you've worked so hard for. Prevent that by always being one step ahead of your competition.

Top tips: How to research your competition

1. **Google is your friend:** As I'm sure you're aware, the internet is an incredibly useful tool. In addition to being able to visit your competitors' websites and research what's being said about them online, you can also set up Google Alerts that will let you know when something has been posted about the company you're tracking.

2. **Speak to your clients**: So often people overlook the most important information source – their clientele! Ask your clients who they worked with before you. Also find out about what led them to stop using those people. Likewise, if a client leaves you, make sure you ask them which company they're going to and why they made that decision.

3. **Attend industry conferences**: Attending a networking function is always a good way to suss out the competition, as you can find out more about them in a neutral environment. You may even discover that you have mutual synergies with them, which might mean you can work together in some way.

4. **Hire people who have worked for your competition**: There's no better way to learn about a company than from someone who has previously worked for them.

5. **Call them**: It may seem like a simple approach, but sometimes simple tactics are the best ones. Simply give one of their sales consultants a call and pretend to be a prospective client. Ask them questions about their business and the services or products that they offer. You'll be amazed at how much you can learn by taking the time to do this.

40

Work Ethic

"Be humble. Be hungry. And always be the hardest working person in the room."
– Dwayne Johnson (American actor, producer,
and semi-retired professional wrestler)

Stop slacking off!

You can't expect to be great at what you do if you're not prepared to put in the required time and effort. Successful entrepreneurs are out there selling, not sleeping! How many times in a day do you lose focus? What you have to realise is that every time you lose focus, you're making it that much harder for yourself to win!

Winners never quit. Winners don't slack off and put things off. Winners get things done. Be a determined competitor. Former United States Secretary of State, George Shultz, had the right idea when he said, *"Winners don't make excuses. The minute you start talking about what you're going to do if you lose, you have lost."*

Be a team player

A company or business is essentially a group of people who work together and form a team. If you look at a football team, for example, you've typically got a squad of about 24 players and only 11 of these footballers will play on the field. Competition for this playing time is tight, and so every day people who are on the squad will compete to be a part of the team on the field. Even though there will be competition, ultimately everyone on the squad will have to work together if they want their team to succeed.

Very often you'll have snipers in a team. These are the negative people who upset the equilibrium of the group. If you aren't a team player, then ultimately everyone will suffer. A lot of people in sales don't realise the importance of being a part of a team. Being a sniper or a lone wolf won't benefit you and it certainly won't help your company. Just like a football team, if you had a centre forward or a goalkeeper who wasn't working with the rest of his team, he wouldn't be able to win the game by himself. If everyone works together, the benefit will be much bigger!

If you can identify people within your team who aren't being team players, then you need to do something about it. It's also possible that *you* might be this person. Sometimes you'll lose focus, go off track and lose your ability to think positively. This kind of negativity will not only work against your own psychology, but your team's psychology too. A team can only win when everyone works together.

A team that can collaborate and move forward as a unit is unstoppable. Never underestimate the power of working together. Remember that it's not all about you; it's about everyone collectively being better, stronger, fitter, and faster, and producing better results, increased revenue, and more sales.

Learn to love the pressure

Some people will tell you that pressure makes them feel anxious, nervous, and uptight, but any great sales professional will tell you that they've learnt to thrive under pressure. Personally, I look forward to pressure because it improves my concentration and motivation. Pressure keeps me on my toes and helps me get things done in a quicker and more efficient way. However, I have also trained many sales professionals who become paralysed when faced with pressure.

If you tend to get clammy hands and feel a knot in your stomach at the thought of looming deadlines, then I'll teach you what I've taught others over the years – pressure, just like fear, exists mainly in your own head. You have the ability to shape it, and if you're open enough to it, then you can use it as a positive driving force.

You might feel pressure from your boss, pressure from your colleagues, pressure from your clients, and pressure from yourself. When you start to let this pressure overwhelm you, simply take a step back and realise that if you're a hard worker who goes about his or her day in the right way, then there is nothing to be stressed about.

The most useful thing that you can do is to reframe the pressure that you feel. Instead of seeing it as a negative, turn it into a positive. Perhaps set a target and reward yourself if you meet it. By controlling how you feel about pressure, you'll find that you'll be more able to take it in your stride.

Top tips: How to turn pressure into a positive

1. **Concentrate on your activity:** Instead of constantly worrying about your outcome, just take it one step at a time and focus wholly on your sales activity. Do your best and concentrate all that you have on getting it done.
2. **Try roleplay:** It's often uncomfortable situations that lead to

pressure. For this reason, it's important to train and roleplay difficult situations on a daily basis. By doing this, you'll get used to thinking on your feet and you'll start to enjoy the thrill of being able to tackle any objection that comes your way.

3. **Maintain complete focus:** When faced with pressure, you should hone in on what needs to get done and be completely focused on getting it done. Multi-tasking won't help you here. Resolve to get one thing done at a time and do not give into any distractions. Only once the task is completed can you move onto other things.

4. **Get it done right:** Often when we feel under pressure, we'll race to get something done. This isn't always the best tactic. Speed can often result in foolish mistakes. What you need to do here is concentrate on getting things done properly. If they're done properly the first time, then you won't need to go back and do it again, which would just lead to more stress.

5. **Use your sales process:** The sales process that I gave you in Chapter Five was designed to help you keep your focus and always stay five steps ahead. If you follow it, then you won't have to worry about what comes next; instead it will be a reflex that will come naturally.

41

Keeping Statistics

"Statistics is the grammar of science."
– Karl Pearson (English mathematician and biostatistician)

How can you expect to grow your business or revenue if you don't know your strengths and weaknesses? Many big companies will implement impressive strategies, but then scratch their heads when they don't get the results they wanted. The problem often isn't the strategy itself, but the fact that these businesses aren't putting in the time to track and assess their sales statistics. Sales statistics can be one of the most valuable tools for a business.

How often do you analyse your own statistics in order to ascertain where you're weak and where you're strong? As I've mentioned before, I'm a person who loves numbers. Without statistics, I wouldn't be where I am today. The Oxford Dictionary defines "statistics" as "The practice or science of collecting and analysing numerical data in large quantities, especially for the purpose of inferring proportions in a whole from those in a representative sample." Simply put, statistics are all the analytical answers that are right in front of you; all you have to do is look!

I keep statistics on every aspect of my life. I always have, and I always will. It's almost impossible to build or accomplish anything without having the correct data. When you track your sales statistics, you'll be able to:

- Understand your strengths and weaknesses;
- Know exactly what needs to be done in order for you to hit your targets;
- Know where you're going wrong and how to fix these problem areas;
- Perform better and achieve your goals.

Understanding your statistics will help you make more informed decisions, and will ultimately lead to more sales and revenue. If you're in the business or sales world, then you're going to have to be more analytical. There is no need to play guessing games when it comes to your career. Data never lies, and tracking your sales statistics could be the difference between making tons of money and none at all.

Let's take a look at some of the basic things that you can track as a sales professional:

- The number of door-knocks that you do;
- The number of people you speak to;
- The number of prospects you meet with;
- Your number of closes that result in clients.

Let's use the following example: If your goal is to get ten new clients every month, then you'll need to know exactly how many people you have to meet with in order to get ten of those prospects over the line.

If you knock on 100 doors every day, and get 50 phone numbers, and 20 of these prospects agree to meet with you, then you'll have 20 new clients – but only if they all sign with you.

If your closing ratio isn't 100%, and you only manage to close one out of every 10 prospects that you meet with, then you would have to increase your door-knocking and meetings with prospects in order to hit your target. From the above example, you would have to meet with 100 prospects to get 10 new clients, and 200 prospects to get 20 clients.

If you keep on tracking your performance in this way, then you'll soon realise what you're doing wrong. In this case, you're not good at closing. If you worked on your closing, then you'd be able to increase your numbers in no time. The benefits of keeping statistics are endless! Most sales professionals will agree that sales is a numbers game, so if you focus on your own numbers you'll be well on your way.

Top tips: What you should be tracking

1. **Your monthly sales:** By tracking the sales that you have made every month, you'll be able to see your progress. For example, if you made 10 sales last month and have made 12 this month, then you know that you're doing well. But if your sales have gone down compared to previous months, then it's obvious that something isn't working.

2. **New vs current customer sales:** Where are most of your sales coming from? A lot of sales professionals are able to upsell their current clients, but others will make more money by closing new clients. Analysing this data will help you to understand where other opportunities for further revenue lie.

42

Time Management

"Until we can manage time, we can manage nothing else."
- Peter F. Drucker (management consultant, educator, and author)

The difference between a good sales professional and a great sales professional often lies with how they use their time and how productive they are at the office.

How often do you find yourself procrastinating during the day? It always baffles me when I walk into an office and see people huddled around the water cooler, chatting in the kitchen, or having a laugh at their colleague's desk. It's called a job for a reason, and if you don't work, then you're not going to get anything done. If your daily routine is overcome with procrastination, then how on earth can you expect to become a success?

The people who spend time gossiping and chatting are always the ones who panic at the end of the day because they can't get their work done in time. This will then result in them having to put in overtime – not because of an excessive workload, but because of their own inability to work constructively. Time management exists for a reason. If you don't manage your time, then it will manage you.

A lack of time management can kill your sales! I've heard a lot of sales professionals moan about the fact that they have no time. They claim that too much of their day is wasted on trivial activities and not enough time is left for the important things. Although a part of sales does require admin work, if you get these activities done early enough in the day, then you'll have plenty of time to tick other important things off on your to-do list.

On every given day at the office there will be interruptions or curveballs that are thrown your way. Plan ahead for these things by setting some time aside in your schedule for any 'unknowns'. If, at the end of the day, you plan your next day's activities in extensive detail, then time will be on your side. One of the biggest mistakes that I see people making all the time is that they take every day as it comes. Instead of planning ahead, they go with the flow. This almost always results in things being forgotten or a mad panic at the end of the day to meet deadlines.

Time management requires discipline. A lot of average salespeople don't spend time on prospecting, calculating statistics, or setting clear and definitive goals.

How do you use the first hour of your day? If you've already got an action list prepared, then you can use the first part of your day to get a great head start on everything. However, if you tend to spend the first hour of your day drinking coffee, catching up with colleagues, and 'settling in', then you're never going to get things done. This is often what separates successful people from unsuccessful people. Be motivated, fired up, and willing to give every task your all from the start of your day until the end of your day.

Top tips: Managing your time effectively

1. **Finish one task at a time:** We've all been told that women are excellent at multitasking, but it's been proven that, regardless of our gender, it's incredibly difficult for people to do two things at the same time. All that you're doing when you multitask is switching between one task and another, which will lead to you losing focus on what's truly important. Instead of doing two different activities at once, group similar activities together and then get them done like that. Once you have completed one task, you can then move on to the next. Working like this will also give you more job satisfaction, as you'll be able to tick things off your list one by one.

2. **Don't take breaks:** Often when people finish one task they'll reward themselves by taking a break. This is not the correct way to do things. All that this will do is break your focus. Instead, keep on going and try to finish as many things as you can in one go. Once you have momentum, don't break it.

3. **Reduce distractions:** Make sure you have your to-do list written in front of you with clear, actionable points. Then block every possible distraction that might come your way. If you're in the habit of checking social media on your phone, then remove the apps from your mobile device. If you know that you're going to get up at some point to get something to eat or drink, then make sure that you have it on your desk before you sit down. Switch your phone to silent, turn off your email notifications, and tell your colleagues that you do not want to be disturbed.

4. **Create templates:** Writing out emails to new prospects can potentially take a lot of time. Instead of writing a new email every time, have a template that you can customise and personalise. Creating templates like this can save a lot of time, energy and effort.

PART VII

Massive Motivation

43

Massive Motivation

"To be a champ, you have to believe in yourself when nobody else will."
– Sugar Ray Robinson (American boxer)

Are you struggling with motivation? Many individuals find it difficult to keep themselves motivated and energised all of the time. I used to believe that it was only lazy people who struggled with motivation, but then I realised that even highly successful people can sometimes battle to keep motivated too.

When you first start a new project, or get involved in something new, chances are you'll feel excitement. This excitement helps keep you motivated. But how do you stay motivated when that initial enthusiasm starts to fade?

There are a lot of other factors that contribute to decreased motivation. Perhaps something has changed in your life and your old goals are no longer that much of a priority to you. Or maybe you experienced failure and now you're discouraged? The trick is to get yourself excited again, and keep on going.

The choice is yours. You can either choose to keep on going, or you can quit. But rest assured that once you quit, you'll never be as motivated as you were before. It's natural to go through a slump here and there, but your attitude determines your outcome. In this chapter, we'll be discussing how to stay motivated and focused!

44

How To Stay Motivated

"When you focus on your problems, you'll have more problems. When you focus on possibilities, you'll have more opportunities."
- Unknown

In the last chapter we discussed the skills that successful people have in common. They're experts in their field, they like to win, they have great attitudes, and they know how to manage their time. But what keeps these people motivated, buzzed and energised?

Exercise

As an active person, I can honestly say that if I didn't exercise each and every day, I would be a truly miserable person. For me, exercise has always gone hand in hand with motivation. If you exercise first thing in the morning, you'll have a clear mind, and a whole lot of endorphins, to help you tackle your day.

There's no excuse for not exercising. Some might claim that they don't have time for such things, but you can always make the time. Cutting down on one hour of sleep in exchange for a healthy body and mind is well worth it.

Make time for your loved ones

You'll hear a lot of professional people who complain about not having enough time with their families. But, just like with exercising, it's important that you actually make time for the people you love.

I have seen so many people in the working environment waste their time during the day, and as a result have to stay late at the office. Of course you're going to miss out on valuable time with your kids if you're not working cleverly. When you're at work, be 100 percent present! Focus on all work-related tasks and get them done in good time so that you can go home to the people you love.

You've got to spend quality time with your family every day. If you control your time carefully, you'll have the chance to do so, and you'll find that it motivates you because your spirit will be lifted by being with the people who you care about most. If you've got young kids, then get up an hour earlier in the morning and spend time with them before you go to the gym and then to work.

Keep your diary full

A happy mind is a busy mind. A full calendar is a great way to keep motivated. Having too much downtime is often the cause of demotivation. Have you ever spent the whole weekend in bed doing a series marathon? How did you feel after doing that? Chances are, you probably felt lethargic and down. Watching TV is not going to help your motivation levels in any way, but engaging with people and getting out and doing things will!

Fill your diary every single day. Seven days a week. The more you're doing, the more energised you'll be! The less you do, the more chance you have of getting into bad habits, and into a negative situation. Doing nothing creates negativity and depression.

Make sure you understand that keeping busy is important. If you do nothing, then you won't see any positive results.

Get a good night's rest

Contrary to popular belief, not everyone needs eight hours of sleep every night. But it is important to find out exactly how many hours your body needs. Some people can survive on four hours of sleep, while others need nine. In my experience, getting to sleep earlier means that I can start the next day earlier.

What is your nightly ritual? Do you spend hours watching television or doing unimportant tasks? If so, then perhaps you should consider going to bed earlier rather than wasting precious hours where you could be sleeping. Let's say, for example, that you need seven hours of sleep. If you go to bed at 9 p.m. then by 4 a.m. you would have already had your seven hours. If you get up at this time, you'll get to see the sunrise, you'll have time to get yourself organised, and you'll get yourself in the zone before anyone else is even awake. There is nothing more energising than being at work before everyone else, and getting a lot done before your colleagues arrive at work.

Try to start your day before the sun rises. It's incredibly motivating. Those two or three hours that you waste staring at the television at night are no good for you anyway. Rather get to bed earlier, get up earlier, and seize the day.

45

Self-Belief

"Your only limit is you."
- Unknown

Wh**hat** would your world look like if you had the ability to shape it and determine its outcomes? Any true leader will tell you that self-belief is key to success. There's no denying the power of self-belief. If you opened up your mind and believed in yourself and in your ideas, where do you think you'd be today?

If you believed that you were incredible and that you had the ability to overcome any hardship or obstacle, then would you be doing what you're currently doing? Probably not, right? This is because the more self-belief you have, the bigger you'll dream and the more risks you'll take.

How would you feel if you had unlimited belief in yourself? And are you willing to step into this version of yourself? Are you ready to become the best possible version of you?

In order for you to truly reach your potential as a sales professional, you'll have to believe in yourself. And I'm not just talking about having a healthy dose of self-confidence. What I'm talking about is a belief system that can't be swayed. A mindset that's able to keep you going no matter what. Having a winning mentality plus determination will give you the power to move forward and produce remarkable results.

Successful sales professionals, regardless of the industry they work in, are able to harness this power of self-belief to assist them in achieving success. Believing in your own ability to reach your full potential is the key.

When I'm faced with a challenge, I look at myself in the mirror and speak through all of my concerns. I tell myself that anything is possible and that I can achieve anything I set my mind to. By having a serious conversation with myself (and I mean serious), I can create my own belief system. Perhaps if you were a bystander watching me do this, you'd probably think I was a little bit crazy, but researchers have identified that talking to yourself is excellent for the brain, and it's also a great trick to boost self-confidence.

Our subconscious is very susceptible to the things we say out loud. The more we verbalise something, the more we believe it. So, when you combine positive statements with looking yourself confidently in the eyes, the results can be amazing. I urge you to give this technique a go. Don't knock it before you try it.

Just Do It

If you let fear rule you, it can keep you from achieving your goals. It's normal to be afraid at times, but what you have to realise is that most of the time, if you give into these fears, all you're going to do is start fuelling the fire of negativity.

If you don't achieve what you set out to do, then you shouldn't be asking yourself why you failed, but rather why you didn't fully believe in yourself. From my experience, if you have conviction, you can do anything. If you truly set your mind to something, there's nothing that can stop you.

About a year ago I went on a trip to an outdoor adventure centre with my daughter, who happens to be terrified of heights. In this particular case, it was bungee jumping. Standing at the top of that platform, she felt petrified, but I refused to let her back down. And then, once she jumped, she ended up doing it another eight times! Because she knew that there was no other option, she faced her fear head on and did amazingly well.

It's the same with sales. Sometimes you need to just jump. Let go of the fear that has been occupying your mind and just go for it. It's a liberating feeling!

Believe In What You're Selling

In addition to believing in yourself, you have to believe in the product that you're selling. Recently a friend of mine, who happens to sell critical illness insurance, beat cancer. Because of what she went through, she truly believes that the product she's selling will make a difference to people's lives, just as it did to hers, and that makes it much easier to sell. If you don't believe in the product you're selling, then how can you sell it? If you can't personally connect with what you're selling and if you don't truly believe that it has any value, then why are you selling it?

Studies show that most 25-year-old men don't believe in critical illness insurance. But after talking to my friend who had cancer, most would now. Always put yourself into the sale. Believe in yourself as much as you believe in the product and it'll make a world of difference.

Do Whatever You Think You Can't

Sometimes, due to many years of preconditioning, our brains can trick us into believing something that may or may not be true. Think back to when you were a kid. Chances are, you didn't like Brussels sprouts – I know I certainly didn't. I thought they were revolting, and even during adulthood I spent many years still avoiding them. Until I had to convince my daughter to eat them, that is, and the only way she'd eat them was if I did too. Lo and behold, when I actually tried them again I realised that they weren't all that bad. Plus, they're healthy. Who would've thought? That same thinking can be applied to other things that your mind controls. You may think that you're a terrible public speaker because you had a few bad experiences in school as a teenager, but in actual fact if you relaxed and used that mirror technique that I was talking about earlier, you'd definitely gain some confidence and have the ability to win over any crowd.

As Nike says: *Just do it*! Do whatever scares you. Do whatever you think you can't do. Because you can make it happen! The proof is in the pudding.

Top tips: Enhancing your self-belief

1. **Don't listen to the naysayers:** A positive mindset will always be better than a negative mindset. If you were to compare any two people, the person with the most conviction is usually the person who succeeds. Don't be swayed by other people's negativity. Remain focused and believe in yourself. Believing in yourself is the only thing that counts!
2. **Prepare yourself for body blows:** I wish I could tell you that the road to success is easy, but it's not. You're going to face rejection and failure along the way; however it's up to you to turn that failure into something positive. Precondition yourself by preparing for setbacks, and then when you encounter problems, you'll know how to handle them.

3. **Know the difference between right and wrong:** If you don't believe in what you're selling, and it goes against who you are and what you believe in, then you shouldn't be selling it. Stay on the path that keeps you motivated and inspired.

46

Do What You Love

"Do it with passion or not at all."
- Rosa Nouchette Carey (writer & novelist)

Working in a job that you hate is soul destroying. Whether you dislike your boss, or loathe your daily tasks, if you don't enjoy what you do you're going to end up living a mediocre and unfulfilling life. People who work just to put food on the table ultimately end up in a position where they have no passion and no pride.

I would never encourage my daughters to work in a job that they don't like. I would never want them to simply earn some money to get by. Every parent wants their child to grow up, take education seriously, and pursue a career that they're passionate about. We want our kids to love what they do for a living. So then why don't we take this advice ourselves? Why do we get up day after day to do jobs that we don't really love?

A lot of people have the mentality that jobs don't have to be fulfilling.

They see their career as a means to an end and something that will allow them to pay the bills. They don't live to work; they work to live. But do you really want to spend the rest of your life hating what you do? Especially if you're going to be doing it for at least eight hours a day, five days a week.

Would you be happy to spend the rest of your life doing what you're doing right now? If not, then what are you doing to change your current situation? What kind of decisions have you made to change it? Of course you need money in order to pay your bills, but I've got news for you – it is in fact possible to make money *and* love what you do for a living. It's important to feel inspired and motivated every day, and to be excited about the day ahead. If you dread the thought of going to work, then you're not doing what you're supposed to be doing!

It's important not to settle for an unfulfilling career. If you take into account the average number of years that a person works before they retire, it would mean settling for 47 years! Why would you waste the majority of your life in a job that doesn't make you happy? A lot of people are stuck in a rut or a routine that they don't know how to get out of. These people fear what would happen if they took any risks to better their situation.

If you fear leaving your job that is bringing in a steady income, then try to do some other type of work or training in the evenings or weekends when you're not working your 9 to 5. By doing this you can re-train yourself, re-educate yourself, and ultimately take the necessary steps in order to achieve your goal and move into a career that you can be proud of. Take the advice that you would give to your kids: get out of the rut that you're currently in, and do something that you're passionate about.

There are so many people out there who do a job that just doesn't fulfil them. All through the week they'll trudge through that job and look forward to the weekend so that they can get away from it. Why would you do what you do if you hate it? If all that you have to look forward to is Friday evening, then something needs to change in your life.

What's the point of disliking your life for five out of seven days? Sunday night shouldn't be a miserable night because you're dreading going to work the next day. When I was a kid I hated school, but back then I didn't have a choice. That's the great thing about having a career; you DO have a choice!

The secret to success is simple: love what you do. Don't just think about what you'd love to do; take action! If you don't take action you'll be stuck in a dead-end job forever. Take action now so that you don't land up living a miserable, mediocre life. When you take action, you'll land up in the place that you want to be. You'll experience the opportunity to grow, you'll feel inspired, and pretty soon work won't feel like *work* at all! You can choose where you want to work, and you can choose what you want to do. Wouldn't you rather be a person who bounces out of bed every day of the week? You should love what you do. And if you don't, then it's time to rethink your plan. Don't settle for a miserable existence! Be passionate about every aspect of your life – including your job.

Top tips: How to love what you do

1. **Take the time to find out what you're passionate about:** In order to do what you really love, you'll need to know what you're passionate about. For me, it was helping others and sharing my knowledge with the world (that's how my business Make-It-Happen was born). After you've come up with a list of things that make you happy, then try to think of ways to turn those things into business opportunities.

2. **Make time:** As with a lot of things in life, if you don't put in the time, then you can't expect results. Once you know what it is that you love and what business opportunities you want to pursue, spend some time mapping out a plan on how you're going to get there. Write everything down and revisit this plan on a daily basis.

3. **Make money from your passions:** If you truly believe in what you are doing, then surely you'll be able to get other people to believe in it too? Brainstorm ways that you can bring in revenue by doing what you love. For example, I do a free Facebook Live stream for my followers every week where I give away advice and tips for free, but then I also have an online university platform that people have to pay for.

4. **Surround yourself with people who believe in you:** Having supportive people in your life will help you to make braver and bolder decisions. Cut all negative people out of your life. If they don't believe in you, then they don't deserve to be in your life.

47

Don't Fear Burnout

"Don't stop when you're tired. Stop when you're done."
- Marilyn Monroe (actress, model, and singer)

People often talk about burnout, but I don't believe in it. In my opinion, if you're passionate about your career, then you won't burn out. If you're truly excited about what you do, then you'll feel motivated to go into work each and every day, and you'll be committed to getting things done.

Think about this for a moment. When you're working on a project or work assignment that you're passionate about, you feel positive and fired up. You don't mind putting in the extra hours. Best of all, if you're positive and energetic, you'll attract more like-minded, optimistic individuals who will want to work with you.

Now turn this scenario around and picture yourself working on something that you hate. You wouldn't be motivated, you wouldn't be energised, and you would resent having to put in any additional hours. With this kind of attitude, people wouldn't want to be around you and inevitably you'd feel quite isolated and depressed. Your clientele would suffer and so would your income.

A lot of people often claim to be burnt out when they're just stressed and no longer able to perform like they once did. But is this a result of an actual burnout or is it simply because they no longer feel fulfilled in what they do for a living?

Do you ever hear about people like Winston Churchill or Albert Einstein suffering from burnout back in the day? No! Working long hours has never been the problem. But not doing what you love is.

When work interferes with your true passions, or when you end up missing the things that are truly important to you, you'll end up being resentful. And resentment is a breeding ground for all the classic symptoms of 'burnout' that people might feel. Feelings of exhaustion and a lack of focus can often be combatted by critically assessing your life and deciding what you really want to be doing with it.

Top tips: How to avoid 'burnout'

1. **Write a priority list:** What's really important to you? What is the one thing that makes you miserable when you don't do it? For me it's exercise, but for you it could be reading, cooking, writing, singing, or painting. Make sure that you block out time in your day for these activities. After checking them off your list, you'll feel less resentful about sitting in the office late at night.

2. **Separate your work life from your private life:** Make a point of finishing your tasks at the office. It may be tempting to take your work home with you, as technology has enabled us to work from almost anywhere. However, this can result in

you feeling as though work is keeping you from your family time. If you get things done at the office in good time, then reward yourself with a night off once in a while.

3. **Go to bed early:** It's easy to lose track of the time when you're working (if you're serious enough about your work that is). Don't underestimate the importance of a good night's sleep! Set an alarm for bedtime if you have to. Going to bed at a reasonable hour will ensure that you're able to think clearly and function at an optimum level at all times.

48

Taking Time off Work

"A vacation is what you take when you can no longer take what you've been taking."
– Earl Wilson (journalist and author)

How much vacation time would you take if you had the option of going on holiday for as long as you liked? Most people love vacations, and I agree that they do serve a purpose. My thinking is that you should take enough time off to fulfil your desire for time off, so you feel rejuvenated and energised.

A lot of folks feel like they need holidays, but if you look at the most successful people in the world, generally they don't take that much vacation time. That's because they don't see their work as a chore; they see it as something they enjoy.

When I go on holiday I'm probably at my most stressed, because I'm away from doing what I love. I usually cut my vacation short by two or three days because I want to get back to work and get stuck into what is helping define my life. That being said, if you need to take time off, then you should definitely take time off. Take three months if need be, until you're bored of it. Then you can get back into the groove of work and get focused.

Use your time off to map out how you're going to achieve your goals. That commitment that you make to your career is going to give you so much positivity and so much energy that you're going to love every single minute of what you do.

A couple of years ago, Richard Branson introduced unlimited vacation time for his staff. "Treat people as human beings, give them that flexibility, and I don't think they'll abuse it. They'll get the job done," Branson announced at the time. This type of policy isn't new, however. Many companies are embracing this kind of thinking. These policies boost morale, increase employee loyalty, and foster more creative thinking. But don't assume that just because companies like Virgin have unlimited vacation policies in place that all their employees are taking holidays all year round.

These vacation policies focus on results. As Richard Branson put it, "It is left to the employee alone to decide if and when he or she feels like taking a few hours, a day, a week or a month off, the assumption being that they are only going to do it when they feel 100 percent comfortable that they and their team are up to date on every project and that their absence will not in any way damage the business – or, for that matter, their careers!"

Even though these employees technically have the opportunity to take months off work, many people won't. But it is up to them whether or not they do, and this in itself is empowering.

Top tips: How to prepare a holiday handover

1. Give advance warning: It's always good to let your colleagues and clients know about your leave well in advance. Check in with all your clients before you take your vacation time and put their minds at ease. Also, be sure to let them know who they can speak to in your absence.

2. Prepare a handover document: Many people leave handover documents until the very last minute and then valuable information and action points are forgotten. Start your handover document at least a week or two before you leave and walk your colleagues through it.

3. Tie up loose ends: Make sure that you do as much work as possible before you go on leave. It might require you working longer hours, but if you want to take leave then you've got to work for it! Make sure that everything is up to date and completed and have clear action points for yourself on your return.

4. Set an 'out of office': What would your prospects and clients think if they sent you a mail and you didn't reply? Ensure that you set an 'out of office' on your email account that includes the dates that you'll be away, the contact names and numbers of the people who can assist your clients in your absence, and an emergency number that they can reach you on should they really need to.

5. Do a handover when you get back: Many people give handovers to colleagues before they go away, but very few receive a handover when they get back. It's important to discuss exactly what happened while you were away so that you know of any urgent action points as soon as you return. Give all of your clients a call to tell them that you're back and ask them what they need assistance with.

PART VIII

Mentors

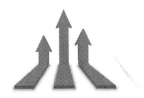

49

Why Mentors Are Important

"A mentor is someone who allows you to see the hope inside yourself."
— Oprah Winfrey (media proprietor, talk show host, actress, producer,
and
philanthropist)

The Oxford Dictionary defines a mentor as, "An experienced person in a company or educational institution who trains and counsels new employees or students". My first mentor happened to be so much more than this, however. In my opinion, a successful mentor has the ability to shape the life of his or her protégé, and that's exactly what my mentor did for me.

I was 19 years old and ready to take on the working world, but I hadn't managed to hang onto a sales job for more than a couple of months at the time. My family had always told me that I'd be good at sales because I had 'the gift of the gab', however, finding the right sales job proved to be a challenge. But then came the day that changed the course of the rest of my life. After a brief stint as a trainee car salesman, I went for an interview with a well-known office equipment company and was interviewed by a man named David Shillingis. He gave me a pen and asked me to sell it to him. I must have said something right because he offered me a job on the spot and the rest as they say, is history.

I was fortunate enough that my mentor had a keen interest in my success, and was willing to teach me tips and tricks that helped me a great deal in the industry. He listened to me and took his time to train me in the areas that I needed help with.

Mentors are extremely beneficial. It's essential to find someone who can coach you. But how do you go about finding the right person to mentor you? They've got to be interested in you, know all about the business that you're in and be prepared to spend time with you on a weekly or monthly basis. Having this kind of support and mentorship can make a massive difference to your career. I know that there are a lot of people out there who might argue that mentors aren't always necessary, but in my experience they can help an average performer become a great success!

My mentor would take time every day to speak to me on the phone. He would ask how my day was, how I was getting on and ask what he could do to help. We would get together once a week and go through all the areas that I was struggling with and he would teach me about sales, business, and life in general. In exchange for lunch and a drink, for two hours every week I had his undivided attention and he taught me a great deal.

I often wonder where I would be today if I hadn't met David. Would I have been as successful if I hadn't had someone helping me along the way?

Many advocates for mentorship will speak about the fact that if you have reached a comfortable level of success yourself, you have the moral obligation to send the elevator back down to those who need some help. Investing your time in someone who truly values your opinion is never a waste. And perhaps the youngster you mentor today could grow up to be the next Richard Branson tomorrow. Everyone deserves a chance. Sadly, however, not everyone is willing to give inexperienced people a shot.

In order to apply for jobs these days, candidates first need to meet a very long list of requirements before they're even considered for the position. Most of these requirements, depending on the seniority of the role, will mention that the candidate should have a minimum of one to three years of experience within that field. The problem with this is that it excludes all of the newbies who have just entered the workforce. These people have youth, excitement, and passion on their side, but because they have no track record, no one believes that they can do the job well. We tend to forget that we all have one thing in common: we were all inexperienced at the start of our career.

And so, in order to get ahead, it's imperative that we form valuable relationships with people. Connections are everything! Also, since most people trust recommendations from people who they know, if you've built some solid relationships, chances are these individuals can refer you to some of their contacts.

50

The Role of a Mentor

"In learning you will teach, in teaching you will learn."
– Phil Collins (singer-songwriter, record producer, and actor)

Mentoring is where one person (the mentor) supports the learning, development, and progress of another person (the mentee). It's the mentor's responsibility to provide the mentee with support by giving them valuable information, advice, and assistance in a way that enables the mentee to advance in their career. Most of us are familiar with the concept of mentoring, but I've met so many people who overlook its potential.

Whether you realise it or not, you have the power to shape someone's life. Wouldn't you want to shape it for the better? Perhaps there is already someone who looks up to you, but you don't realise what a difference you could be making. Now there may be some selfish sods out there thinking, "But what's in it for me?" Well, let's get one thing straight. If you want to be a mentor, then you have to be one for the right reasons. You have to be selfless at times.

However, mentoring isn't just about empowering other people; it's also a source of self-learning and personal growth. It offers you the opportunity to make a tangible difference to the success of others. Perhaps you'll help build their confidence, support their career growth, or just help them get a foot in the door. Soon, you'll find yourself enjoying the difference that you can make to someone's life, and your happiness will skyrocket as a result.

A mentor is someone who is able to take on the role of a trusted adviser, supporter, and teacher to another person. The relationship is most effective when you focus clearly on the needs, goals, and challenges of the person you are mentoring. It's therefore important to map out how the relationship will work prior to you starting to mentor someone. Clearly define what they expect from you, and what you expect from them.

51

A Culture of Success

"Show me a successful individual and I'll show you someone who had real positive influences in his or her life. I don't care what you do for a living – if you do it well I'm sure there was someone cheering you on or showing the way. A mentor."
— Denzel Washington (actor, director, and producer)

Think back to the person that you were when you first got started in your career. Would you say that you're still the same person you are today? I certainly hope not! That's because we learn, and we grow. We experience hardships and failures, as well as successes and triumphs. Each of these experiences has the potential to mould and shape us, but more so than anything, the people who we come into contact with on our professional journey will have the biggest effect on us.

Mentors and managers have the ability to make or break an individual. With the right encouragement and support, an average salesperson can become a great salesperson. After all, if you had someone who believed in you and who was rooting for you, you'd believe in yourself too, right?

Over 80% of employees believe that they would benefit from a mentoring programme. Research has also proven that mentoring programmes boost employee engagement, foster new career development, and create new leaders. It's a wonder then that not all companies offer this opportunity to their employees.

Creating a culture of success within your business starts with creating a culture of success with your employees. Motivate them, listen to them, and steer them in the right direction. If you do this for your employees, in return they'll give you their loyalty, and that is priceless these days.

Likewise, if you're a newbie salesperson who wants to be successful in his or her career, then make an effort to speak to the right people within your organisation about possible mentorship opportunities. A lot of employees have this bizarre notion that they can't speak frankly to their employers. Many people seem to think that it's best to keep a low profile at the office, but you will never advance within your company by doing this.

If you want to make a good impression, then you've got to be proactive. Ask if your company has a mentorship programme. If they don't, then ask your boss if they would mind you picking their brain and learning from some of their successes. If you ask nicely, and if you're genuinely interested, then your boss is unlikely to turn you away. Showing interest and being teachable is a very positive attribute in the working world.

Be Prepared To Put in The Effort

I've spoken before about how my mentor at work provided training to a group of us from 6 a.m. until 07:30 a.m. every morning. The job was in London, so it meant me waking up at 04:30 a.m. and leaving my house no later than 5 a.m. every day. If you weren't at the training on time, then you weren't allowed in, but because I found the training so inspiring, I was always front and centre.

The best mentors are the ones who have a vested interest in their mentees, and David always made a point of checking in on me every day. That's not to say that he wasn't pushing me and working me hard, however. As I said previously in this book, every day I had to knock on 100 company doors and get 100 introductions. Then, once I got back to the office, I had to call each of these 100 people and try and get a meeting with every single one of them. I was always the first one in the office and the last one out. This was my life for 18 months, and at the end of those 18 months, I was the only trainee still standing. To this day, I'm still very proud of that fact. If you aren't prepared to put in the effort, then don't expect to get anywhere in life. A successful life is a hard-working life.

Why Businesses Are Embracing Mentorship

Today, more and more businesses are latching onto the concept of using mentoring as a professional development tool. By empowering young staff members, businesses are seeing a dramatic improvement in productivity and efficiency. I've mentored thousands of young sales professionals over the years and many of them have gone on to become hugely successful millionaires. I've always believed in giving back, and that's part of the reason I started Make-It-Happen University. Behind every successful person, there's a mentor who helped them along the way, and seeing people succeed makes me truly happy.

Thirteen years ago, I employed a young lady by the name of Danielle Suchley. At the time she was doing sales and manning the telephones, but I recognised something unique in her. She had such incredible drive, and I just knew that she'd be massively successful one day. I took her under my wing and promoted her to various different roles over the years. Today she is the Managing Director of the Blue Sky Thinking Group, which is a $50-million business.

When I see something special in one of my employees, I do whatever I can to further them and their development. I do this without expecting anything in return, but perhaps this is one of the big reasons why my staff stay loyal to me. When both parties are able to work together, and they support each other and push one another to be better, that's where the real magic happens.

Millennials In The Working World

There has been a shift in the working world in the last few years, and a lot of people who I coach come to me for advice regarding clashes between leadership and their millennial staff. Millennials generally tend to be uncomfortable with rigid corporate structures and expect career growth to come quickly and easily. A new report published by PwC reveals that most millennials are constantly on the lookout for new opportunities and that very few are interested in staying in the same field and progressing with one company. This means that employers are going to have a tough time attracting and retaining talent in this day and age.

I might be generalising here, but in my opinion millennials want a management style and corporate culture that is very different from anything that has come before. They demand that their needs and wants be fulfilled, and if they don't feel valued, they'll leave their company without thinking twice about it. If there's not something in it for them, then they won't feel any loyalty towards you or your organisation.

For example, I recently received an email from an MD in Scotland who was struggling with managing the millennials within his organisation:

Hi Spencer
I've got a bit of a management problem within my sales team at the moment. Many of our staff members are quite young and inexperienced, but instead of being eager to

learn, they've become quite arrogant and believe that they should be handed things on a silver platter. I came down on a few of them last week and told them that if they're not prepared to work, then I'd show them the door. But now the office morale is down and it's not helping their performance. Do you have any advice on how we can motivate our young team to want to be better?

This question got me thinking. Millennials have a ton of positive attributes, such as their ambition and desire to keep growing. But they do tend to have egos and are only interested in doing things if they get something in return.

A lot of sales companies struggle with their staff, and what they often do really wrong is that they just want to fill the positions, instead of understanding what kind of person that they're actually looking for. Do you know exactly the type of person who you want to employ, and who would be a great fit for your organisation? If not, it's important that you map this out immediately and stop hiring people who look good in a suit and simply say the right things in an interview.

If you have staff who are ungrateful and unwilling to put in the effort, then get rid of them as soon as possible. If you don't, they'll start to influence other people within your company, and eventually they'll take over and rule the roost – after all, they already think that they do. While it's important to motivate, inspire, and reward good work, I don't think that it's necessary to pander to people's egos all the time. If they're not interested in putting in the work, then they shouldn't be there. It really is that simple. Finding the correct people to fit your business will take more time, but it'll be worth it in the long run.

Since most millennials want to feel that the work they do is valuable, it makes more sense to clearly explain what your business is about when you hire people, and make sure that they find the work that you do to be important. If a person is just taking a job for the money, then their heart will never be in it, and they'll soon be on the lookout for another, better opportunity. But if they feel that they can make a difference within your organisation, then they might have an incentive to stay for longer.

Famous Mentors

Some of the most influential people were mentored. For example, a lot of people don't know this, but former Apple CEO Steve Jobs was a mentor to Facebook CEO Mark Zuckerberg. During the early days of Facebook, the two often met to discuss the best business practices for the company.

Queen of talk, Oprah Winfrey, also had a mentor in celebrated author and poet, Maya Angelou. She has often spoken about the benefits of mentorship, saying, *"Mentors are important and I don't think anybody makes it in the world without some form of mentorship."*

The Makings Of A Mentor

What makes a good mentor? Well, a good mentor needs to be more than just a successful individual. He or she should also have the desire and drive to actively develop other people. If you truly want to inspire other people, you'll also have to reflect and share your own experiences, including your failures.

While it's worth noting that a mentor is not an oracle who has the answers to everything, it's vital that they have in interest in doing everything in their power to help develop their mentee.

Top tips: How to be a great mentor

1. **Have a desire to develop and help others:** Even though

the relationship between a mentor and his or her protégé is a two-way street, as a mentor you've got to be willing to give of your time and resources without expecting anything back.

2. **Devote commitment, time, and energy to the mentoring relationship:** A mentor's relationship with his or her protégé isn't a quick thing. It's a relationship that develops over time. Be prepared to put in the hours.

3. **Have current and relevant knowledge, expertise, and skills:** You wouldn't take parenting advice from someone without a child, right? In order to be a successful mentor, you'll need to be able to talk the talk and walk the walk.

4. **Be willing to share failures and personal experiences:** Mentors need to communicate both their 'how I did it right' and their 'how I did it wrong' stories. Both types of experiences provide valuable opportunities for insight and learning.

5. **Cultivate a learning attitude:** Because a mentor is more like a teacher than a coach, learning is an important characteristic in a mentor.

The Perfect Protégé

Just like there are characteristics that make a successful mentor, there are also certain traits that make a good protégé. Effort, appreciation, dedication, and a whole lot of drive are at the top of my list, but there are other kinds of behaviour that will help you benefit from your relationship with your mentor.

Top tips: How to be a great protégé

1. **Be willing to ask for help:** I've met a lot of people who want to do things their way and don't want to accept advice from others. I was also like this before I met my mentor. I thought I knew it all, when in fact I didn't really know anything at the time. Respect people who have been in the

field for longer than you. Ask them questions and learn from their success stories. You won't be sorry!

2. **Be ready to try new ideas:** It's never easy stepping out of your comfort zone, but don't expect to get a new result by doing the same thing. Mentors are there to offer suggestions. Try as many of their ideas as you can.

3. **Have the ability to accept constructive criticism:** I'm the kind of person who says it how it is. If you want to grow, then you'll have to stop being offended and start using the constructive criticism to your benefit!

4. **Be personally responsible and accountable:** The only person responsible for you is you! Blaming others will never get you far in the workforce. Be honest with your mentor. Don't use excuses.

5. **Commit to meeting on a regular basis:** Just like you can't expect to lose weight without cutting out certain foods, you can't expect to learn from your mentor if you aren't there to take notes. I met with my mentor every single day for more than 18 months. It paid off big time for me, so imagine what it could do for you.

If you don't have a mentor right now, then think about where you could find someone suitable. Ask your friends, family, or colleagues if they know of a suitable person. Having a mentor helped shape my life for the better and I'm certain that having a positive figure in your life helping you along will do wonders for your career too!

PART IX

Overcoming Failures

52

What I've Learnt from Failure

"Success is not final, failure is not fatal: it is the courage to continue that counts."
– Winston Churchill (British politician, army officer, and writer)

Tons of people speak about success, but very few speak openly about what it tends to do to you as a person. The more you have, the more you want. Over the years I became more and more successful, but with that success came arrogance. I was one of the best wealth managers in the international arena, and I started thinking that I was above other people. I felt invincible. I believed that I would never experience failure. There's a well-known saying, *"The higher you climb, the further you fall"*. But I never thought that I would fall … until I did.

I was knocked down to earth with an almighty crash when my CEO – the guy who I'd helped build a business with – decided that he didn't want to carry the business forward with me any longer. Although I had been at the company for 16 years, he no longer thought that I was the right person for the job.

As if losing my job wasn't enough of a blow, the following day I was informed that I needed spinal surgery. It was also around this time that my partner told me that she didn't want to be in a relationship with me anymore. In just a few days, I experienced three massive blows. I went from having everything and living the high life to having almost nothing.

This sent me to a very dark place. I wasn't even sure whether I wanted to continue living. I'd had enough of the world and I hadn't accepted the fact that I was actually responsible for what had happened. The wind was knocked out of my sails for a long time after this.

It was during this time that I stopped believing in myself. I was depressed and in a downward spiral. But then one day I had a realisation. As much as my failures were affecting me, I realised that I owed it to myself and to my kids to pull myself together. I sat down and decided that I had to do something about it. I told myself that it couldn't get worse than it already was at that point. The only way to go was forward and up.

I took a notepad and pen and went and sat in a place that had a nice view of the countryside and I wrote down what I was going to do. I looked at what I really wanted to achieve and then gave myself just one small task to complete that day. That first day I took one step, then the next day I took another one, and a week later I was making those little steps every day. The following week I started taking two steps a day, and so it continued.

I learnt something incredibly valuable by doing this. I realised that you can overcome any failure and any setback that you're facing. The trick is that you've just got to do it slowly, and little by little.

I also learnt just how important it is to be surrounded by the right people. My family and close friends helped me a great deal during that rough patch in my life. They gave me hope and made me realise that there was in fact lots to live for. My kids kept me grounded, and my now-wife Anna and my friends, Danielle and Sarah, were very support-ive. They were there for me when I needed it the most.

When you look at your life and see the wonderful people you have around you, it gives you a reason to re-focus. In my case it allowed me to pick myself up and face the right direction and actually look forward to my future.

The experience that I went through gave me the opportunity for a new beginning. It made me identify what it was that I really wanted to do.

It's quite simple: if you want to have the life that you dream about, then you've got to change your story. Remove the excuses, because if you change your story, you'll change your outcome. And if you change your outcome, you'll have a much better life.

Sometimes failure is a good thing. It'll give you the wake-up-call that you need and will force you to remove all the things in your life that are doing you no good. You might think that people will judge you for fail-ing, but the reality is that you'll be judged more if you let that failure get the better of you.

If you want to be great, then you've got to do great things. But don't scare yourself into thinking that you have to achieve everything overnight. Slow and steady wins the race. Take your time and keep moving forward, bit by bit, until you reach your destination.

53

Is Fear Causing You To Fail?

"Fear is temporary, but regret lasts forever."
- Unknown

Fear. Few words are as powerful as this one. But why? It's just a four-letter word! I've interviewed a lot of successful people on my Facebook channel, and I always ask them what they think keeps people from achieving their dreams. They all have the same answer: fear. Fear is what prevents people from succeeding. Fear of failure, fear of the unknown, and the fear of not knowing how to do something.

Do you remember how you felt when you finished school? I felt completely liberated! Most youngsters believe that the world is their oyster and they are genuinely excited about their future. They want to live their best lives and achieve great things, but more often than not, if you fast-forward ten years down the line, you'll find that most of these people have settled for mediocre jobs and mediocre lives. Why? Because people are terrified of failure!

The moment you experience your first dose of failure something changes in the wiring of your brain – either it forces you to try harder, or it makes you stop trying and simply settle. Sadly, the latter is the case for most people. Fear is one of the biggest obstacles keeping you from achieving massive success! If everything you want is on the other side of fear, then surely it's worth overcoming?

Many people desperately crave change, and yet they're too terrified to take the necessary steps to change their situation.

That's the sad reality about comfort zones; they keep you glued to your very average existence and will rob you of any chance of a better life. Nothing ever grows in a comfort zone! It may feel safe, but it's the black hole of life. It steals your creativity, it destroys your dreams, and it zaps your ambition!

If you want to be a successful person, you'll have to realise that change is inevitable and very necessary in order for businesses to survive and thrive. Fear can stop us from doing great things. For example, fear of failure or losing money often holds people back from becoming entre-preneurs and going out on their own. If I had let this kind of irrational fear stand in the way of me starting my first business, I wouldn't be where I am today.

If you want to live a life that you truly love, then it's imperative to take action. You're also going to have to take some risks. Granted, some risks will be bigger than others, but if you're not prepared to give everything that you've got, then you'll never be happy with the outcome.

I'm not saying that you should blow your life savings on a whim. But I am encouraging you to think long and hard about what it is that you want to do with your life, and then I want you to go after what truly makes you happy with everything that you've got.

In order to achieve your goals, you'll have to move past your fear. A quick way to assess whether you really want something is to imagine yourself when you are 80 years old, nearing the end of your life, having not achieved any of your dreams. What are your regrets? What do you wish you had made more time for? What do you wish you had tried? What would make you feel this way?

The only thing scarier than failure is regret. Chances are, if you think you'll regret anything later on in life, then you shouldn't be letting anything stand in your way of doing that thing.

We all make excuses: "There's just not enough time", "I don't have the money or the resources to start my own business", and "I'm just too busy". We hide behind these excuses because they're safe. But as I've already said, nothing great ever happens when you're stuck in the safe zone. Every time you find yourself making excuses, stop! Hold yourself accountable and stop limiting your progress by playing it safe.

The most successful people are the ones who believe in themselves and believe in fostering a growth mindset. People often give up on what they want because they think that reaching their goal is beyond their abilities. The next time you're faced with a challenge, think of your abilities as flexible, rather than fixed. Think of this challenge as an opportunity to adopt a new strategy.

Failure, disappointment, and dead-ends can help refine what it is that you really want. These can all be used as a means of reflecting and saying, "This didn't work. How can I make it work better?" Remember that fear is only in your mind. Humans are built to adapt and deal with failure and diversions. Use each experience as a tool to help you learn more about yourself and what you really want.

Failure isn't actually as scary as you think. It may sound bizarre to you, but the best cure for your fear is the realisation that you will fail. Any successful person will agree that it's just part of the process. Failure offers insights and inherently corrects the faulty ways of approaching a problem. There is no teacher as impactful as the sting of failure. Use these experiences to adjust your strategy and start again.

54

Rationalise Your Fear

"Fear: False Evidence Appearing Real."
- Unknown

W hat exactly is it that you're scared of? The quickest way to overcome your fear is to understand it. If you're afraid of your business failing, take a few steps back and start visualising all the positives. Write down everything that scares you and then next to those negatives note the positives. The more you do something, the easier it becomes. That's why it's important to do what scares you. Do something that scares you each and every day. Start with small things and work your way up to bigger things. Stop overthinking and just do it! You'll soon wonder what it was that you were ever afraid of.

While failure is inevitably a part of every job, in sales you might face quite a bit of rejection. In this chapter I'm going to teach you how to overcome such failures.

The biggest mistake that you can make is being too scared to make any mistakes. Fear is one of the biggest underlying causes of failure. Fear makes you fail, before you've even had the chance to get properly started.

Top tips: Overcoming four common fears

1. **Not believing in yourself:** Low self-esteem and low confidence can stand in the way of you believing that you can do something and really deliver. This belief system can cause many problems. A great way to build confidence is to focus on the little wins. Small wins can help you feel good about yourself and remind you that you're getting somewhere.

2. **Believing that everything needs to be perfect:** I often see people thinking that everything needs to be perfect before they go into business. But what if something was good yet profitable, instead of being perfect and not profitable? It's really important that you get going on your journey rather than waiting for perfection. You can always learn along the way.

3. **The need for financial investment:** People often fear that they don't have enough money to start their business. But you'd be surprised at the number of people and resources that are out there if you just hustle a bit more than you currently do. Put the time and effort in. Learn and gather information from family, friends, coaches, and mentors. You'll soon discover that there are a lot of things that you can do without money. There are loads of free resources online, for example. Get stuck in and do as much as you can without depending on the revenue first.

4. **A lack of experience:** Many individuals may worry that they don't have the right amount of experience to be a great entrepreneur. But the reality is that every successful entrepreneur has to start somewhere. They may not have had the experience or the knowledge when they started out, but they learnt as they went along. The best lessons and the best experience that you can get is by trying and doing.

55

A Bit of Pressure Is Good for You

"When the going gets tough, the tough get going."
- Joseph P. Kennedy (American businessman, investor, and politician)

Y ou would have heard the saying "If you can't handle the heat, then get out of the kitchen". Well, if you can't handle pressure, then you shouldn't be in sales!

Many people claim that they don't deal well with pressure. I, on the other hand, thrive under pressure. Pressure is what pushes me and motivates me to keep going. Most successful salespeople will agree that they enjoy the adrenaline of a challenge, and the thrill of hitting their targets. Learning how to handle pressure is one of the most important things that you can do for your career and for your own mental health and well-being.

The more pressure I'm under, the better! I always map out my goals and targets, examine what I've got to do, and then set about getting everything done one thing at a time.

Be honest for a minute. When are you most motivated and fired up? When you've got tons of prospects, tons of clients, and tons of work? Or when it's dead quiet and you have nothing to do and nothing to fill your day with? It's always when you've got too much free time that you start questioning things. You question yourself, question your career choice, and question your job.

Want to know the simple trick to feeling motivated in the workplace? Keep busy! Give yourself things to do. Even if your boss isn't putting pressure on you, put pressure on yourself. Soon you'll be getting things done faster than anyone else in the office, and you'll be hitting your targets quicker than any of your competitors.

Top tips: How to handle pressure

1. See the value of pressure: Instead of panicking and worrying about not being able to handle your current situation, see the pressure that you're under as an opportunity for growth. Believe that you can overcome any challenge that comes your way and learn how to use pressure as a positive instead of a negative.

2. Focus on the positives: Stand in the mirror and say all of the things that you're great at out loud. Positive affirmation is scientifically proven to enhance self-confidence and boost your results.

3. Focus on what's important: Instead of getting bogged down by the details, focus instead on the fundamentals. List the things that you need to get done in order of importance. Then systematically work through that list until you've completed each task.

56

Common Sales Failures

"Success is the ability to go from failure to failure without losing your enthusiasm."
– Winston Churchill (British politician, army officer, and writer)

L et's get just one thing clear: everybody messes up at some point in his or her career. Mistakes are inevitable, but if you learn from them, then you can prevent them from happening again.

Very early on in my career I made a massive mistake that cost me dearly. I tried to encourage my prospect, which was a university, to buy my product by offering them a shopping trip to New York as an incentive. They were incredibly insulted by this offer and told me that they would never do business with me as a result. So I had to learn the hard way, but I never made that mistake again.

Apart from making these kinds of errors, there are many other, simpler reasons that can lead to a salesperson losing out on a sale. Over the years I've met so many sales professionals who make the mistake of not asking for business. These people don't close their prospects; they might go through all the steps but at the end of the process, they don't ask for the business. It might seem nuts that salespeople wouldn't ask their prospects for the business after putting in all the work, but at the end of the day it comes down to the fear of rejection.

A lot of us have an inbuilt fear of getting a 'no'. You might not want to push your prospect too hard and risk losing the deal, but if you don't ask for the business you're probably not going to get it anyway. I would rather my prospects said 'no', than nothing at all.

57

Top Reasons Why Closes Fail

E very good salesperson will learn dozens of closing techniques. But sometimes, they'll still fail to close. Below I've outlined some of the most common reasons for sales professionals losing out on big deals.

Pressure And Persistence

The difference between pressure and persistence is something that confuses a lot of salespeople. It's also one of the most common reasons why these sales professionals aren't hitting their sales targets.

If you believe in your product, your company, and your service, then you're not pressurising your prospect by insisting you close the deal. It's not pressurising people when it's the right thing for them to do. In these cases, it's actually your responsibility to get the deal done and to make the sale. However, if you're selling a product that you know isn't beneficial for your prospect, then you shouldn't be forcing and pressurising them.

Not Believing

Many people fail to close because they don't believe in the product they're selling. It's hard to convince a prospect about something that you don't personally care about. Whether you're selling cars, office equipment, or financial services, if you're not passionate about your product, then your prospect will see through your façade.

Either get engaged with the product you're selling, or find something that you really believe in that you can sell. The positive impact of believing in what you do and what you sell will help you consistently close all the time.

This is why some employers will demand that you eat, sleep, and breathe their brand if your job is to sell it to others. Just imagine what kind of message it would send to the world if the CEO of BMW refused to drive a BMW in his day-to-day life. That's exactly the same as a financial advisor selling a retirement plan to one of his clients that he wouldn't personally invest in himself or recommend to his closest friends and family. By selling something, it automatically makes you an ambassador for that brand, so it's your responsibility to believe in that product and its value.

Incorrect Assessment

Another reason why some salespeople fail to close is that they don't accurately assess the amount of effort needed in order to be effective. People who have grand ideas and fantastic goals often don't achieve success because they don't execute their plans properly. This is because they either don't put the right amount of effort in, or they don't have the relevant skills to achieve their goals.

If you're an average salesperson who only closes one in five sales, and you want to up your ratio to four in five, then you'll need to assess the skills that you have currently and then enhance the skills that you'll need in order to up your closing ratio.

For example, if you don't know everything that you can possibly know about the product or service that you're selling, then you simply haven't put enough effort in. If your client were to ask a question about your product or service that you were unable to answer, then they wouldn't have much confidence in you going forward.

In order to be a successful sales professional, you're going to have to commit to putting a great deal of effort in and learning all the skills required. You've got to have a plan, a structure, and a strategy.

Not Having Financial Targets

It's really important to have a financial plan in place. Many salespeople have a budget and they know what their expenditure is, but they haven't worked out exactly how much money they want to make or set a timeline for when they would like to hit their financial targets.

Without a financial plan, how are you going to get buzzed and motivated? Without goals, you won't have any urgency to achieve the things that you need to. And if you don't have urgency, then you're not going to close business deals. If you're going from meeting to meeting with the mindset that you only need to close enough deals to pay your monthly bills, then you're never going to be a great sales professional.

I often hear newbie salespeople complaining about a commission-based income, but I would much rather have a commission-based income than something set in stone. For me it's never been about simply covering my monthly bills. I've always thought far into the future and wanted more. With a commission-based income, you can accumulate massive revenue each month, but in order to be super successful, you'll have to have a target and work according to your own personal financial plan.

If you have to get up and go to work every day, then surely you'd want to do better than just coast by? Wouldn't you want to achieve wealth and the kind of life that you dream about?

The only difference between people who have a lot of nice things and people who don't is goals and massive action. Successful people make a conscious decision to pursue something with everything they've got. These people have financial objectives and a solid plan in place. This helps them to stay motivated to get things done.

It's essential to have a plan: where you are today, what you want to achieve in the future, and how you're going to go about getting there. Then look at this plan every single day to track your progress and inspire you to attain those goals.

Top tips: How to budget like a pro

1. **Work out what your expenses are:** It's important to know your exact monthly expenses, so that you can save the rest of your income each month. Once you've worked out how much you should be saving, set up a monthly debit order that will automatically transfer this money into a savings account.
2. **Make sure that you don't have easy access to your savings:** By putting a 90-day access on your savings, you'll think twice before withdrawing from this account.
3. **Know what you're saving for:** What are you saving for? Your retirement? A house? Your kids' education? Whatever it is, you probably know when you need that money by, so break it down so that you know exactly how much you should be

saving each month. For example, if you want to save $100,000 within five years, then you need to save approximately $1,670 every month in order to hit that target. Do the maths! It's a simple method and will help you a lot in the long run.

Blaming External Factors

Many salespeople tend to blame external factors when they fail to make the sale. They blame their prospect, they blame their product, and they blame their company.

Someone once told me: "No matter where you go, there you are". This made me realise that a lot of the problems that I faced when I was younger weren't caused by external factors, but were actually because of me. I was the common denominator. And, until I realised that, I wouldn't be able to do anything to fix the situations that were causing me hardship.

You will continue to make mistakes and encounter problems until you take responsibility for your own actions. You're going to lose business if you hold other people accountable. Take responsibility, and if something goes wrong, then learn from it.

People will respect you a hell of a lot more if you apologise and take responsibility for your actions, as opposed to you blaming external factors. Your attitude determines your outcome. Remember that!

Thinking A Complaint Is An Objection

Taking a complaint for an objection when it's not can be the reason why you aren't managing to close a deal. Many sales books that I've read over the years don't differentiate between complaints and objections. You should treat everything as a complaint until it's validated otherwise. Nine out of ten times, people aren't objecting; they're just complaining, and just because they're complaining, it doesn't mean that you have to do anything with that complaint.

So when your prospect says that the price of your product is too high, treat it like a complaint. Say something along the lines of: *"Yes it is high, but it's a great product and worth your money. Shall we get the paperwork done?"* If a complaint becomes an objection, then address it, but don't see every complaint as an objection. Acknowledge the complaint and move on.

58

How To Handle Rejection

"Achievers reject rejection."
- Lolly Daskal (leadership executive coach and keynote speaker)

I've shared how I managed to overcome failure in my personal and professional life, and how to manage fear. I've also talked about some of the most common causes of sales failures and what leads to many failed closes, but what I haven't spoken about in detail is how to handle rejection. This topic goes hand in hand with fear. People often fear rejection even more than they fear failure.

Rejection is something that many people struggle with, but it's made so much worse when it's blown out of proportion. Let's think about it like this. When you're young and single, it's inevitable that you will face some kind of rejection when approaching people you're interested in. I definitely wasn't always a charmer, and had to learn from a few awkward encounters how to get better responses from the girls who I liked. Any person reading this right now has had to deal with some sort of rejection from someone they were keen on. You might walk away with a dented ego, and it may slow you down a bit, but it won't stop you from putting yourself out there again and giving it another go.

You'll think about different ways to approach a situation, so that you don't get the same negative response or outcome.

When youngsters enter the working world, they're mostly ambitious and are excited to learn. But what happens when these people experience their first real dose of rejection at work? Some salespeople might eat up that rejection, spit it out, and move on. But others might allow that rejection to really affect them, where they get themselves into a certain state of mind and can't handle anyone saying "no" to them.

If, for example, a prospect were to say "no" to a salesperson's product pitch, it would be extremely painful for them. Inevitably, these people will stop seeking out prospects, purely because the fear of rejection and the fear of hearing "no" are too great.

Sometimes we allow a problem to become bigger and bigger in our own minds, until we reach the point of it becoming absolutely debilitating. Your mind creates all sorts of negative scenarios in your head. If you go into a sale believing that your prospect isn't going to buy your product, then you've already lost. You might as well not even go into that meeting.

Let's think about rejection in the world of sales for a minute. If someone says "no", then is this rejection really an attack on you personally? Some people believe that it is. But what you should be thinking in this scenario is that perhaps what you're presenting isn't appealing to your prospect. Perhaps your proposition isn't the right one for them, or maybe they're just not interested in the product that you're selling.

I've seen people who are terrified of picking up the phone. It's like they think something is going to come through the phone and eat them alive! Or at least that's the impression that they give others watching them. The fear of what the outcome might be is so insurmountable, that they don't want to make a simple phone call to a prospective client.

Back in the eighties when I was a newbie salesperson, my boss told me that for every 100 cold calls I made, I would get 99 people who would say "no". He also told me that while not all of these people would be rude to me, some would. Some might swear, some might hang up, and some might tell you to bugger off. But one out of these 100 people would inevitably say "yes". If the 100th person you call buys your product or service, then what is this person worth to you? If you've got a goal that you're working towards, then you'll know that getting through the 99 "noes" every day is just a part of the job. All those "noes" will be worth it at the end of the day when you eventually get your "yes".

It's important for you to decide whether or not the commission from that one "yes" will be worth going through the rejection of the 99 "noes". For me this was a no-brainer. You need "noes" and you need rejection. Rejection will do two important things for you – it will toughen you up and it will teach you new skills.

Every time that someone rejects you, think about the things that you can do to limit the number of "noes" you get going forward. Think about how you can better yourself or improve the way that you're presenting your products or services.

Tons of people claim to have tried everything, and still received the same negative results, but this is absolute rubbish. Trying four or five different approaches does not mean that you've tried everything. There are plenty of benefits to getting rejected. A "no" today can lead to two "yeses" tomorrow if you just change your approach.

You will encounter many highs and lows in the world of sales. If you let the lows, which are the "noes", impact you negatively, then you'll never experience the highs, which are the "yeses".

If you accept that you need to go and find "noes" in order to find the "yeses", it will allow you the opportunity to perceive rejection very differently.

Entrepreneurs or people with start-ups will all tell you that rejection is part of the game. Banks will refuse to fund you, corporates will shoot down your ideas, and people might not believe in you, but you've got to go through all those "noes" in order to find the "yeses". And when someone says "yes", it will be a sweet, sweet victory.

PART X

Sales Behaviour

59

The Reality of Sales

"The art of conversation lies in the listening."
- Malcolm Forbes (American entrepreneur)

We've worked through quite a bit in this book. I introduced you to the exciting world of sales, we learnt how to prospect, we spoke about the role that digital media plays in this industry, and we focused on how to set clear and definitive goals. I then took you through the four gears of the sales process, we spoke about all the skills needed for success in sales as well as in life, and we learnt how to build an environment for success.

In Chapter Nine we dived into all of the reasons why salespeople fail and how you can overcome those failures. In this chapter, I'll be focusing on sales behaviour and how to use everything that you've learnt in this book to boost your performance and keep on winning.

If you're new to the world of sales and are reading this book as a start, then I hope that at this point we can agree that the world of sales isn't as daunting as you had initially thought. Yes, you have to work hard, but that's the same as with anything in life. If you're prepared to put in massive effort, then you'll be rewarded with massive results.

Can you imagine making over $20,000,000 in direct sales? What would your life look like? And how would it feel to be known as the go-to person in your industry? If you can see it, you can do it!

60

Truly Understanding Your Audience and Consumer Behaviour

"If you want to know how to sell more, then it's essential to know why people buy."
– Unknown

In Chapter Three I spoke about the importance of having a social media strategy in place for your business. Before digital media completely changed the way we communicate, we spent more time getting to know others in person. If anyone wanted to find out more about your business, then they would most likely call you up and arrange a meeting.

But these days, the very first place people go when doing research about your business is digital media. Potential customers will usually visit your website and then move on to your social media pages. If you're not doing a good enough job of selling yourself and your services on these platforms, then you're going to miss out on a ton of business. People will also be checking the recommendations from customers on your social media pages, so if you don't have enough of these, or if you're not engaging with your followers, it will show.

I'm sure that you've heard the term "influencers" being used in digital media circles in the past few years. Influencers are people on social media who have built a massive following by providing content that others are interested in. It's now possible to make a ton of money by being a beauty or travel blogger, for example, if you build up a following and get the right brands to endorse or sponsor you. Many of these bloggers now have more influence than modern celebrities or politicians. Why? Because their followers are interested in their opinions and will buy the products or experiences that they suggest. In a recent study conducted byTapInfluence and Nielsen Catalina Solutions, it was shown that influencer marketing generates 11 times more ROI (return on investment) than traditional forms of marketing.

If, for example, you were a successful travel blogger, then a partnership with an airline like Emirates would be ideal. You would blog about your great experiences with the airline, and then your followers would definitely consider using Emirates when planning a trip. People follow the recommendations of individuals who they trust, and if you're an influencer on social media, then tons of people will take your advice to heart.

Where many people or wannabe-influencers go wrong, however, is trying to be everything to everyone. It's so important to have a niche or a focus. If you're a beauty blogger, then write about beauty products. If you've successfully built your audience by sharing your preferences in lipsticks, then don't suddenly start posting about motorbikes.

Likewise, if you were trying to become influential in the world of real estate, you wouldn't start posting about your body progress at the gym or your cooking talents. Different audiences exist for different people. Know what your audience wants. These days there are so many resources and tools that allow you to map out your audience and give you insight into their interests and likes. On Facebook, for example, you're able to see demographics such as the age and gender of your followers.

Once you know what your audience is interested in, give them more of that! Regularly check in with them to make sure that they're enjoying your content. If they're not engaging with your content, then change it. There's no sense in pushing out 20 self-help videos a week on Facebook or YouTube if no one is watching them, sharing them with their friends, or talking about them.

What's also important when trying to influence people in the social media world is not to be too pushy or too "salesy". In a nutshell? Don't be annoying. People never respond well to spam!

Say the word "salesperson" to most consumers and they'll scrunch up their faces, roll their eyes, and run for the hills. The number one reason why people don't like door-to-door salespeople or telemarketers comes down to the simple fact that people don't like to feel pressured. Very few people enjoy the 'in-your-face' approach. And so if this approach doesn't work in person, then why would it work on social media?

Facebook, Instagram, and Twitter are all littered with in-your-face advertisements and lots of pop-ups begging you to click on their page, which can come across as quite desperate.

So how do you get around this? How can you get people to opt into your messaging and follow your pages for the right reasons? I would advise that you stop making sales pitches and start conversations instead. Since most people love talking about themselves, it makes sense that they'd want to join conversations that they are interested in and can engage with. While it's hard to initially grab someone's full atten-tion in the cluttered social media space, once you have it, you'll find that these people will eagerly share their opinions with you. Keep sharing great content, keep giving them unique insight and advice, and keep engaging with them.

Being genuinely interested in your followers' opinions will show. What do your followers get from your social media pages? Are you educating them? Are you helping them make more informed decisions? Are you entertaining them? Make sure that your audience is getting something of value each and every time you post.

Just as understanding your target market on social media is vital, so is understanding the psychology of the buyer who you're meeting with in person. We discussed in Chapter Nine how to assess why your prospect might be hesitant about signing with you, and how you can gently nudge them along. As I mentioned, it's important to know the difference between an objection, a complaint, and a straight-up 'no'.

Instead of memorising lines about the services you offer, the products you sell, and the company you work for, you should engage with your prospective client in conversation that flows naturally. While scripts are very popular in telemarketing businesses, they won't necessarily help you when it comes to meeting someone face to face.

In order to ascertain whether you can be of value to your prospect, you need to listen to everything that they're telling you, study their body language, and gauge their level of interest. Essentially, you need to know and understand your prospect, and where they're coming from.

Each person has their own interests and set of needs, so unless you find out what your prospect wants, you are never going to find common ground with them. If you're genuinely interested in people, it will show.

And if you give people what they want, then you'll be well on your way to building a good business relationship with them.

What keeps your prospect up at night? What do they worry about regarding the future? What concerns do they have that you can help them with? How can you make them happier or more at ease? Listen to their problems so that you can help them find solutions to those problems. Once you've heard everything that they have to say, make them visualise how much better their business or personal life would be with your assistance. You're there to help ease their burden, after all.

Top tips: Understanding your audience and target market

1. **Understand the problems that you can solve:** List all of the problems that your product or service can address. Once you've done this, it will give you a clearer understanding of the person who you are targeting.

2. **Ask yourself questions about your target market:** Is the person who I'm targeting married? What job do they do? What is their net income? How is my product going to help them? The 'spray and pray' approach just doesn't work anymore. This approach is when you reach out to a mass audience without any clear strategy and just hope that one or two of them will buy your product or service. If you're going to be solving real problems, then you need to be painting a picture of real people with real needs. Once you have your ideal avatar, you'll find it a lot easier to target the people who would actually be interested in doing business with you. Why? Because your product was designed for them!

3. **Know what your company does best:** Do you have particular areas of expertise? What are your USPs (unique selling points)? Do you get along better with certain types of people? Knowing these things is vital when working on defining your target market. For example, if you were a single

party guy who doesn't like kids, then you wouldn't do very well selling educational plans to parents. Use your knowledge and your skillset to your advantage here.

4. **Know what else is out there:** Once you've answered all the above questions, and you know what type of person you're targeting and how you can help them, do some research on other products in the market. When you've done a comparison between those products and yours, add some unique features to your products that people won't be able to find anywhere else. For example, if you're selling family vehicles, then include some educational books or something else of value that your target market would appreciate. It's the little details like this that will set you apart from the rest.

61

Working Your Way up the Ladder

"Behaviour is the mirror in which everyone shows their image."
– Johann Wolfgang von Goethe (German writer and statesman)

I f you're the CEO of a company and are reading this right now, then I'm sure you would agree with me that if one of your employees actually took the time to arrange a sit down with you to discuss how they can go about doing their job much better, you'd be quite impressed by them.

Whenever I get asked how newbie salespeople should go about working their way up the career ladder, I advise them to go and sit with their employer to chat about exactly what they want or need you to do. Discuss setting and achieving quantitative goals, for example sales targets and profit margins, and qualitative goals, such as personal development and commitment. Once you know what's expected of you, go and execute those tasks as quickly and as efficiently as possible. If you keep on doing this, your boss will soon realise that you mean business and will give you more tasks and responsibilities as you go along. It really is as simple as that.

Take initiative, do things that aren't in your job description, and work hard. When you go above and beyond what's expected of you, you land up proving your worth within an organisation. What you need to do is get to the point where you're doing so much for your employer, that they would find it hard to ever replace you. Once you've achieved this, you'll be able to discuss promotions or career advancements more openly and you won't be overlooked if you've genuinely been working hard and putting in the right amount of effort.

It's actually quite a simple strategy when you think about what you have to do in order to move up in the business and sales world. Sadly, there are some individuals who have been stuck at the same level in their company for years. But what it all comes down to is initiative. If you don't volunteer and don't get stuck into making things happen for yourself, then no one else will do it on your behalf. So many salespeople can get stuck in a rut if they're not careful.

I've met many successful business owners who land up losing everything they once had because they start becoming complacent and stop putting in the required work. Businesses don't run themselves and your career won't continue to thrive just because you've experienced success in the past. Sometimes employers should take a page out of their employees' book and also take the time to ask how they can be better.

Make a point of having one-on-one meetings with your employees to catch up with them, find out how things are going, and what you can improve on in the workplace environment. When your staff feel appreciated and heard, it will show in their performance. Your staff retention will also be higher, and you won't have to spend as much money on recruitment. Checking in on your employees' progress consistently will help in achieving the overall business strategy, as well as growth and financial targets.

In addition to this, you should regularly set aside time to brainstorm new ideas and strategies that will keep your business thriving. Those top performing companies are the ones that are always one step ahead of everyone else in terms of new ideas and innovation.

Top tips: How to work your way up the ladder within your organisation

1. **Have a good relationship with your boss:** Fact: the people who get promotions are the people who are well known and liked by their employer. Make sure that you're likeable, do things that make your boss' job easier, and touch base frequently. Don't wait until your boss asks you for a report; do it ahead of schedule and send it to them. Also, try to touch base with your boss about any new ideas or opportunities that you have for the business. This will show them that you take initiative and that you're on their side.

2. **Share your accomplishments:** If you've done a good job, won an award, brought in new business or made a client extremely happy, then share this news with your boss! Keeping proof of all of your accomplishments is necessary when you're trying to work your way up the corporate ladder. Next time you get a complimentary email, forward it to your manager saying something along the lines of: "Thought you'd like to see that Mr Jones finally came around and signed with us. He's happy to be working with our company and his business has just added X amount to our company's revenue!" Sending an email like this lets your boss see how external stakeholders value you.

3. **Step up:** If you want to get ahead quickly, then you have to be a yes man! Arrive at the office early, always be the first to volunteer to take on new projects, and be a dependable team player at all times. All bosses love their employees to be go-getters.

4. **Maintain integrity:** Don't be the person in the office who blames other people when things go wrong. If you had a part to play, then be honest and accept responsibility. Likewise, be prepared to share credit. Giving credit where it's due will win your colleagues over, and prove that you've got integrity.

62

Getting the Best Partner

"Great things in business are never done by one person;
they are done by a team of people."
– Steve Jobs (American entrepreneur, business magnate, inventor,
industrial designer, and co-founder of Apple Inc.)

Life always centres around relationships, doesn't it? If you want to be happy, then you've got to have the right friends. If you want to love and be loved, you have to have the right boyfriend, girlfriend, wife, or husband. If you want to feel appreciated, then you need to find the right boss, and if you want your business to thrive, then you have to find the right business partner.

Life and relationships go hand in hand. And I'm sure that you know what happens when you've got toxic people or relationships in your life. I've had to cut many people out of my life who weren't influencing me in a positive way – clients, friends, and employees.

A partnership is like a marriage, and if you want to prevent a messy divorce, it's imperative that you don't settle for the first person who comes your way.

I've had my fair share of businesses and have had many business part-ners. If I've learnt anything, it's that you need to know them really well. It's not good enough for them to tell you about the things that they've achieved; you need proof of this. You also need to spend time with them in order to ascertain who they really are, especially in trying circumstances. A person will obviously react differently in a stress-free environment, compared to when the pressure is on.

Just like the people who I hire, I always have an exact avatar of who I want my business partners to be. For me, the perfect business partner is someone who complements my skills and also has skills that I don't have. I've worked with one of my current business partners, Danielle, for over 12 years now, and we both believe in the same goal. We might think about business differently, but at the end of the day we believe in the same outcome and because of this, we have really valuable commu-nication.

The perfect business partner is someone who you can trust 100%. If I didn't trust Danielle and she didn't trust me completely, then our busi-ness relationship just wouldn't work. I would never get into business with someone who I didn't know. I take a long time getting to know a person inside and out and I make a point of being aware of their track record before committing to anything. In addition to these things, it's also important to be able to have fun together. Business is tough some-times, so if you can have fun, then it will make the hard times easier to get through.

Top tips: How to find the best business partner

1. **Make sure that you've worked together before:** If you've worked together before, even if it was 10 years ago in different roles, you would know how the person responds in times of stress and pressure. You would have also spent a lot of

time with them and it's always a good idea to work with someone who you know you want to be around.

2. **Share the same values:** Finding someone who you can connect with and who has the same values as you will do wonders for a business relationship. You can have different views on certain topics – that's life – but if you can agree on the things that are truly important, such as trust, honesty, and work ethic, then you'll be okay.

3. **Have the same goal:** Just as it's imperative to have someone who has the same values as you, it's important to be on the same page when it comes to goals for the business. This is usually what leads to a parting of ways in terms of business partnerships – when partners can't agree on what it is that they ultimately want for the company. Differing views won't help here. You need to share the same goal.

4. **Have strengths that complement one another:** Whatever you lack, your business partner should make up for. I often see two people going into business together where one has the idea, and the other person has the funds, but it needs to be more than this. Perhaps you're great at strategy and they're great at implementation. Or perhaps you're good with relationship building and they're good with keeping the businesses financials on track. Make sure that you both know what you're good at and what you're not so that roles and responsibilities will be clearly defined.

5. **Share the risk:** Find someone willing to take on the same risk as you. A person who is completely invested is more likely to give more of themselves in terms of time, energy, and resources, and is less likely to leave you hanging or make you do all the work.

63

Daily Rituals

"The secret of your future is hidden in your daily routine."
– Mike Murdock (singer-songwriter and televangelist)

I'm quite open about how I go about my daily life. If you've watched any of my YouTube or Facebook videos, then you'd know that I'm a bit of a workaholic (it also helps that I love what I do), and that I live for new challenges.

I recently hosted a sales training seminar and many of the passionate young salespeople attending wanted me to share a bit of my daily routine. I know that while some people are creatures of habit when it comes to their own routines and prefer to live by the motto, "If it's not broken, don't fix it", I do think that we should all reassess how we go about our daily rituals in order to determine whether or not ours needs tweaking.

According to the Oxford Dictionary, the word "routine" refers to a sequence of actions regularly followed. So if you wake up early for only three days of the week, then this doesn't really constitute a proper routine. I follow the same morning ritual every single day:

4:30 a.m. I wake up

5:00 a.m. - 6:30 a.m. I train at the gym (or outdoors if the weather permits)

6:30 a.m. - 7:30 a.m. I shower, get ready for work, read the news, and eat breakfast.

7:45 a.m. I arrive at the office and write my to-do-list for the day. I always use two sheets of paper and I write a detailed list of all the tasks that I've got to get done. I then use the second sheet of paper to rewrite all of those tasks, listing the worst ones first so that I can get them over and done with.

I work in 15-minute slots, instead of hour by hour. So I divide the things that I need to get done into these bite-sized chunks. This allows me to be more effective with my time because I know that I've only got 15 minutes to get each task done.

It may seem self-explanatory, but the importance of a daily ritual such as the one that I follow not only does wonders for your productivity levels, but also for your mental health. Your habits influence every single aspect of your life. I'm willing to bet that I'd be able to figure out what type of person you are based solely on the time that you get up each morning and the number of tasks that you get done in the first few hours of each day.

Some may assume that following a set routine is like functioning on autopilot. People who are more creative may not like working like this. But one's daily routine is a choice or a whole series of choices that shapes the course of your future.

If you're a chronic procrastinator who struggles to stick to a regular schedule, you'll find it more and more difficult as time goes by to get things done. Due to advancements in technology, a lot of people are now working from home. These people may believe that they'll be more focused at home, away from the distractions of co-workers, but it takes an extremely determined and disciplined individual to actually be able to work remotely.

How do you go about your normal day at the office? And what do you do when you've got a deadline to meet? If you're one of those people who spends time tidying up your cubicle, making coffee, surfing the internet for inspiration, and essentially wasting your day, then you join about 89% of the population. It's easy to see then why only a minority of people are truly successful.

Instead of simply going with the flow, I encourage you to map out a schedule that you'll be able to follow. Once you get started, it'll become easier and easier to follow. Take for example the trivial task of brushing your teeth in the morning after you wake up and at night before you go to bed. We all do this every day (or at least I hope that's the case), and we don't have to actively think about it. We just do it. It's as natural as breathing. And with time, you'll be able to achieve other productive tasks just as easily.

Top tips: How to create a daily routine that works for you

1. **Set your alarm clock for the same time every day:**
   This includes weekends! Just because it's the weekend, doesn't mean that you should waste the precious time that you have by sleeping the day away. By doing this, your body clock will soon adapt and you'll never have a blue Monday again, especially since every day will start the same way.
2. **Make your bed:** I know that I've mentioned this before, but

by making your bed every day, you automatically wire your brain into knowing that it's go-time! There will be no temptation to get back into bed, and you would have started the day on the correct footing. Having a cleaner is no excuse for not making your own bed!

3. **Make a list of your daily tasks:** After you've exercised, eaten breakfast, and arrived at work, write out your to-do list. Then rewrite this list from the most difficult tasks down to the easiest tasks. Executing all those things will be a lot easier and you'll have more energy to handle all those ad-hoc tasks that come your way during the course of the day.

4. **Write out a weekly schedule:** Stick this schedule on your fridge, on your mirror, or somewhere that you are guaranteed to see it daily.

5. **Go to bed at the same time every night:** If you want to wake up at a decent hour in the morning, then you need to go to bed at the same time every evening. I don't care if *Game of Thrones* is on! Getting some shuteye is way more important than staring at the TV.

64

Dominate Every Challenge.
Every Obstacle. Everything

"Each of us is what we are because of the dominating thoughts we permit to occupy our minds."
– Napoleon Hill (American author)

I'm sure that if you are in sales you would have heard the saying, "Why compete when you can dominate?" In today's world, it's simply not good enough to just coast by. You have to be the best. You have to achieve amazing things. You have to dominate! But many people struggle with the concept of dominating. They think that it's an aggressive approach and not easily attainable.

But being someone who dominates in life isn't a bad thing at all. It shows resilience, strength, and determination. A winning attitude and mentality is everything! And guess what? Dominating the competition is actually quite simple. You dominate by being the person who works the hardest for the longest. You can lead in any industry and any market if you work harder and more effectively than your competition because your competition won't be able to keep up with the strides that you keep on making.

But this also means that you can't rest when your competition is resting. It means that you can't take holidays when everyone else is on vacation, and it means that you have to keep on going, even if you encounter many hardships along the way.

People who dominate in life are stronger, tougher, and more committed than anybody else. No matter what a person's background, if they're 100% committed to achieving their dream, they can!

I recently interviewed a woman by the name of Maria Conceicao and was incredibly moved by her inspiring story. It all started in 2005 when Maria visited a slum in Bangladesh while on a 24-hour break as a part of her job with Emirates Airline. The desperate struggle that the kids in these slums face on a daily basis made a huge impression on Maria, and as a result she started the Maria Cristina Foundation, with the aim of providing education to the children in those slums.

It wasn't an easy feat getting funding for this organisation, so Maria decided to do incredible things in order to get people's attention. Despite having no previous athletic ability, in the past few years Maria has summited Mount Kilimanjaro, made a successful trek to the North Pole, and walked a marathon on each of the seven Emirates in the UAE in seven days.

In 2013 she became the first Portuguese woman to summit Mount Everest and since then has run seven ultra-marathons on seven continents in six weeks, seven ultra-marathons in seven days, and seven marathons on seven continents in 11 days. She holds six Guinness World Records and shows no signs of slowing down.

When personal trainers told her that she couldn't achieve these ambitious feats, she remained committed to not only pushing through each challenge, but also dominating each and every trial that came her way. And because of her 'can-do' mindset, she's managed to educate over 600 children to date!

As you can see from the story above, having a dominating mindset isn't a cocky or arrogant thing. It's about accepting a challenge and being committed to being the best possible version of you. It's a 'never-say-no' attitude. It's wanting to be the best. It's believing in yourself when other people don't. It's winning!

I was quite similar to Maria when I started off in the business world. If anyone told me that I couldn't achieve something, I was that much more committed to dominating the task. I've never liked to lose and if it means me working harder than anybody else on the planet to win, then I will!

Top tips: How to dominate in the business world

1. **Be prepared to do what others won't do:** An easy way to dominate in the business world is to do what your competitors aren't willing to do. For example, some sales companies close at precisely 5 p.m. every day and they don't meet with clients outside of normal working hours. Making yourself available to your clients 24/7 will make them feel valued and supported. Not everyone is prepared to give out their cellphone number, or agree to evening meetings, but if this can separate you from your competition and allow you to dominate the market, then it's well worth doing.

2. **Be the person who everyone goes to for advice:** Yet another reason to be on social media is to position yourself as the go-to person for tips on topics relating to your industry. When I first started my Facebook page, I was committed to providing valuable insight for FREE to my followers. Within a

few months, I'd built up a following of 50,000 people who came to me for advice on sales and business. Positioning myself in this way has further helped me dominate the market in Dubai, as not many other sales trainers have been prepared to do this.

3. **Set new challenges for yourself:** The only way to dominate is to constantly push yourself and do new things. It's imperative to think differently. Look at what everyone else is doing and then do something unique. And if someone tells you that something can't be done, prove him or her wrong!

65

Accept Criticism

"Learn how to take criticism seriously, but not personally."
- Hillary Clinton (American politician)

D o you remember what I said about criticism in Chapter Six? If you're not open to constructive criticism, then you're not open to truly growing as a person.

One of my biggest pet peeves is people who get easily offended. Unfortunately, millennials are now famous for complaining about feeling offended, but you know what? If you're upset *that* easily by what someone says to you, then you're clearly not cut out for this industry, or any industry for that matter.

Being able to accept criticism is part of being a grown up. I love it when people give me constructive feedback! While it's sometimes tough to hear, it helps you better yourself and your situation. Not everyone will like you, and you won't always receive praise for the things that you do. But I'd much rather be saved by a bit of criticism than live my life in a delusional bubble.

If you want to succeed in life, both professionally and personally, then you need to learn how to take criticism in your stride. Hearing people's opinions is an invaluable tool that has the ability to strengthen relationships, improve your performance, and see you achieving new goals.

Top tips: How to handle criticism like a pro!

1. **Establish whether the criticism is positive or negative:** There are tons of reasons why people may offer criticism. Perhaps your boss wants you to improve your work, your wife wants your relationship to flourish, or your colleague just wants the best for you. Sometimes as much as the truth can hurt, we need to hear it. But there are exceptions when it comes to criticism. If a person is disparaging you in an attempt to break you down because they are jealous of your success, you should not accept it. Not all feedback is constructive, and it will be pretty clear when it isn't. I've mentioned before how important it is to cut negative people out of your life, and if certain people are always tearing you down, then cut your losses and remove them from your life. However, if there is some merit to what the person is saying, then listen to them.

2. **Stay calm:** It's easy to become defensive when someone is criticising you. But if you don't remain calm, you won't hear what it is that they have to say. Listen objectively. Once they are finished saying what they have to say, then respond, but do so in a non-emotional way.

3. **Listen:** Just as I stated above, if you don't listen to what the person offering you feedback has to say, then you won't be able to make any positive changes. Instead of getting defensive, listen to how their advice can help you. At the end of the day no one is perfect, but if you're committed to bettering yourself, then you'll be well on your way.

4. **Don't take anything personally:** Who cares if someone doesn't like your product? Likewise, if your boss calls you lazy,

then use this as an opportunity to become the opposite of that. Sinking into a depression over what people say to you won't be beneficial in any way. Hear it, process it, learn from it, and then move on. It's as simple as that.

5. **Have an outlet:** Effectively managing your stress is very important when you're in the business world. Have you noticed that you're more likely to fly off the handle or take things personally when you're rattled or stressed? Alleviating stress by means of exercise, meditation, or whatever else works for you will help you to remain cool, calm, and collected.

66

Get Out and Do It

"Start embracing the life that is calling you. Find your calling. Know what sparks the light in you so you – in your own way – can illuminate the world."
– Oprah Winfrey (American media proprietor, talk show host, actress, producer, and philanthropist)

I f you take anything away from reading this book, I hope that it's made you realise that if you truly want to make a success of your life, then you've got to get out there and make it happen! The time is now! Not next year, not next month, not tomorrow; NOW!

I've personally made over $20,000,000 in direct sales, won more awards than you can imagine, and have successfully coached thousands of other salespeople to achieve millionaire status; but I can only help people who want to be helped.

What does success mean to you? A lot of people confuse success with money, but there's more to success than just that. Money won't make you happy. You might think it will, but it won't. The more you have, the more you want. It's sadly the human condition to always want more. So few of us are grateful for what we have until it's gone.

What truly makes you happy? And what kind of legacy do you want to leave behind when you die? No one gets out of this life alive, so why aren't we all pushing to live the best possible life that we can? Why aren't we all striving to do our best? We should all aim to be the best possible versions of ourselves. We should be living a life that we can truly be proud of. We should be leaving behind a legacy. In my opinion, this is what it means to be truly successful - to live without regret, to give everything 100%, to make the most of every opportunity that comes your way, and to commit to making things happen for yourself.

If I told you that you were going to die next month, how would that make you feel? Would it make you wonder about how different every-thing could have been if you'd done all those things that you had wanted to do? Would it make you work harder, faster, and smarter so that you could provide for your loved ones after you're gone? Or would it make you realise just how many opportunities you've lost out on because you waited on the sidelines your whole life?

If you dread going to work every day, then you're doing the wrong thing. If you're constantly broke and struggling to make ends meet, you're also doing the wrong thing. I want you to realise that you can be anything that you want to be. If that means being the best salesperson on the planet, then be that person. But don't just do it for the money. Do it for a reason. Do it for a purpose.

I work not because I have to, but because I want to. I was fortunate enough to make most of my money in my twenties and thirties. But now that I'm in my forties, I'm more determined than ever to live a life that I'm proud of. I want to live a life that my family is proud of too. And I want to help others feel fulfilled in what they're doing with their lives.

Get a piece of paper and quickly jot down everything that you've got going for yourself. These are all the things that you're grateful for, such as your house, your family, your job, etc. Now write down all the positive attributes about yourself, such as your work ethic, your determination, your motivation, etc. These are your strengths. Now write down all the things that you want to be that you aren't now. For example, if you're smart but you're not driven, then write that down. Now write down all the things that make you happy. This could be sports, music, people, etc. Now write down what you want to achieve, but make sure that you combine it with the things that make you most happy. If for example, you listed sport, then what are you doing to make sport feature more prominently in your life? Perhaps you could think about selling something related to sport, since that's a natural fit for you. Do you see where I'm going with this? Design the life that you want, and then live it!

Set clear and definitive goals with action steps next to each and every point that you listed, and then make a promise to yourself that you're going to be 100% committed to achieving everything that you want, and then more. You need to get motivated and fired up about the future. If you are a sales professional without motivation, your idea won't matter, your product won't matter, and you won't take action. So many people struggle with that motivating driving force, but we all have an incentive that lights us up. Never lose sight of that.

If you're struggling with the inspiration to get up in the morning, then you're clearly not thinking about your incentives enough. When I was in school I struggled to get excited and I couldn't stay focused. But when I started thinking about all of the things that I was going to achieve –note that I didn't say the things I *wanted* to achieve but the things I was *going* to achieve – then I became insanely motivated.

I wanted to become a millionaire, so I became one. I wanted to be the best salesperson in the world, so I won the Global Salesperson of the

Year Award several times. I wanted to climb Everest, so I did. I wanted to start a university and teach others how to sell, so I did. Every single thing that I've ever wanted to do, I've done. I know without a shadow of a doubt that I can do anything that I set my mind to. Motivation, determination, and a 'can-do' attitude ensure that I never lose sight of my goals. And you should never lose sight of yours.

Make-It-Happen University

"Success occurs when your dreams get bigger than your excuses."
– Spencer Lodge

Because you purchased this book, I'd like to offer you a 25% discount on my online sales training programme. If you're ready to take your career to the next level, then I strongly recommend signing up today.

Visit https://learn.makeithappen.university/ and use the promo code *making-it-happen*.

Make-It-Happen University teaches you all the tools you need to break through your barriers, smash through your sales targets and achieve massive success. Whether you're an employee who wants to learn how to be a better salesperson through our leadership programme, or a CEO who wants to cultivate a strong sales and leadership culture in the workplace, Make-It-Happen University has the tools that you'll need to help you on your way. Transform your sales team, redefine your success strategy, and realise that you can achieve anything you set your mind to.

I'd love to hear your feedback

If you'd like to get in touch, you're welcome to send an email to **sl@make-it-happen.com**, or you can call me on +971(0)505 565 063.